I Went to Kindergarten in Casablanca

A Memoir

GILDA ZIRINSKY

I Went to Kindergarten in Casablanca

Copyright © 2025 by Gilda Zirinsky

All rights reserved.

Published by Red Penguin Books

Bellersose Village, New York

ISBN

Digital 978-1-63777-755-8

Print 978-1-63777-768-8

No part of this book may be reproduced in any form or by any electronic or mechanical means, including information storage and retrieval systems, without written permission from the author, except for the use of brief quotations in a book review.

I dedicate this book to my resilient, brave, and loving parents, Gisa and Abraham "Poppa Abe," Miller.

Contents

1. Warplanes Overhead	1
2. Gisa and Abraham	8
3. Caraman, France	22
4. On Route to Bayonne	28
5. Sunny Casablanca	37
6. Coming to America	42
7. A New Land	49
8. Newfound Family in America	56
9. Latchkey Kid	64
10. Back to Europe	75
11. Back to School	86
12. Our Israeli Adventure	91
13. Moving to Suburbia	107
14. My American Idol	112
15. Losing Ronnie	116
16. Reparations Trip	126
17. The Joys of Being a Grandmother	132
18. The Patriarch and the Matriarch Die	139
19. My Return to Casablanca	145
Epilogue	147
Acknowledgments	153

ONE

Warplanes Overhead

My most vivid memory of my early childhood began when I heard enemy planes flying overhead in Liege, Belgium, where I was born. It was May 10, 1940, and I was just two months shy of my fifth birthday. It was late at night, and the roaring engines of planes in the dark night frightened me, and I cried.

I'm sure my parents tried to comfort me. *What child could comprehend what was happening?* There were planes flying all around us as my mother and father scurried about trying to put together some of our belongings in the rush to get out of our house. Emotionally, they were ready to go. That past September, German forces had invaded Poland. It was a joint attack by Nazi Germany, the Slovak Republic, and the Soviet Union, marking the beginning of World War II.

Anticipating the war would come to our city, my parents had rented a small room near Dunkirk, France, with their friends Rika and Karl Gittman, who had a young daughter, Stella, who was around my age. They paid a year's rent in advance and stocked it with food in preparation for a long stay. They had chosen the location because it was close enough to England to be able to travel there if the war came to this part of France. But amid the panic of the German air attack, my parents could not recall the exact location of the rental and abandoned the plan. Bombs were already falling on Liege, and we were beginning to hear reports of the first casualties in the area.

My parents opted instead to leave Liege on the next train, no matter the destination. Before departing, my mother went around to the home of our good friends, Bernard and Sala Rotzstain, who also had an eleven-year-old daughter, Esther. My mother wanted to tell them we were fleeing and recommend that they accompany us out of the city. But they declined, believing they were not at risk. With little hope of changing their minds, my mother returned home to finish packing, but she could not leave in good conscience without trying to persuade them one last time. So, she made a second visit to their house in the minutes before our departure, and to her relief, she was able to convince Bernard and Sala to heed her warning.

Sala even offered my mother a bit of advice, suggesting that she take the family's valuable silverware with her. In wartime, treasures can be even more valuable than cash. Of course, amid all the excitement, my mother left the silverware behind, along with most of her other things. She cared more about the family's safety than any possessions that we might have had.

I silently watched as my mother hurriedly packed one bag for each of us. She put mine, a small *rucksack* (backpack), on my back and filled it with warm underwear and clothes that I might need, together with my identification papers in case we were separated. She also put in some *Côte d'Or* chocolate bars in case I needed a snack. She loved chocolate, and *Côte d'Or* was her favorite.

In her suitcase, she placed a fur wrap for warmth and a few dresses, mostly made of crepe de chine (silk). I desperately wanted her to take one of the beautiful evening gowns she had sewn by hand. I loved that dress. It was hot pink taffeta with a black tulle overskirt adorned with large silk flowers, a Cinderella-style dress. Of course, she left it behind. I did convince her, however, to take a box of family photos; they would turn out to be the only memories of our life in Liege.

As we gathered by the front door, I cried that I wanted to take my kitten with us. But that wasn't an option. We just left a dish of milk and bread in the backyard and hoped she might somehow survive. I was near hysterics when my mother sternly announced, "We're going!" and directed us to follow her out the door.

My father, who had built a successful tailoring business with many employees, just locked the door to his shop that day, never to return. What a hard decision it must have been to leave everything he had worked for behind and somehow believe that we would be able to start all over again somewhere else.

Under the cover of darkness, we hurried to the metro station. Our odyssey felt like a scene from a movie, terrifying and fraught with angst. Bombs were dropping, and people were running in the streets and screaming. The station was crammed with desperate souls, but somehow, we managed to board the last train to depart Liege that night.

Just minutes after we pulled out of the terminal, the station was bombed. Dozens were killed, and hundreds were stranded. The attack on our city–known to Belgians as the "18 Days' Campaign"– was part of a broader offensive by the Nazis that included the invasion of Luxembourg, the Netherlands, and Belgium, and marked the start of the long expected westward invasion.

At barely five years old, I had no idea what was happening, why we were running, and from whom. To then, our life in Liege had been happy and peaceful. My father had a successful business, we lived in a lovely apartment, we had lots of friends, and we were part of a close-knit Jewish community. But in what felt like an instant, all that was gone, and we were fleeing for our lives. It was only later that I learned of the rising tide of antisemitism spreading across Europe.

Being so young, my memory of our journey out of Liege is spotty. Thankfully, many years later, my son Kenny interviewed my parents about our ordeal, capturing a verbal documentation of the whole story in my mother's words. Remarkably, her recollection began with the story of our train ride out of Liege that fateful night.

She recounted that we stayed on that train for what seemed an eternity as it wound its way west, away from Liege and closer to our destination of Tournai, a small Belgian city near the French border. Our goal was to cross into France, where we hoped we would be safe.

Once in Tournai, my mother sent a telegram to her eldest brother, Hersh, who lived in Brussels with his wife and eight children, urging him to pack up the family and meet us at the border. Hersh was hesitant at first. He was a butcher, just like his father and grandfather before him, and he and my mother were particularly close.

He owned his own shop in a busy part of Brussels, and he and his large family of ten, he, his wife and their eight children, all lived in a two-bedroom apartment in the back of the store.

Concerned that they were no longer safe, my mother implored her brother to leave the city at once.

Gilda's Belgian identity card, 1939.

But with ten mouths to feed, he could not afford to just close up shop. Telegrams went back and forth, with my mother begging him to reconsider and promising that she and my father would help them as best they could. Realizing the danger facing them, Hersh agreed to meet us in Tournai.

We waited in Tournai for three days for them to arrive. When the family finally deboarded the train, we noticed they were now a party of eleven. Hersh's eldest daughter, Gusta, was newly engaged, and her fiancé, Max, was traveling with them. It was a happy reunion, but our joy was quickly overshadowed by the news they shared. They told us they had to leave Brussels in a hurry, as the Germans were advancing on the city in their march west toward France. On May 18th, the German air force attacked civilian targets in Brussels as the German army marched through the city. Hersh and his family had gotten out just in time.

It was clear we needed to keep moving, so we boarded a train for Caraman, a small town in southwestern France, not far from Toulouse, with the hope of eventually making our way to England. We were now a party of fourteen travelling together.

The journey was long, and during the trip, the train made several stops to take on water for the steam-driven locomotive. It was powered by coal, so the crew had to constantly shovel coal into the firebox. I remember watching the steam rise from the engine and the hissing sound it made as it was being exhausted through the smoke stack.

During one stop, members of the Red Cross boarded the train with food. When my mother asked for fourteen sandwiches, the Red Cross worker balked, explaining there was a limit of one sandwich per person.

"But we are fourteen people," my mother said.

"No one has fourteen people in one family," the worker replied.

But my mother would not give up. She invited the volunteer to come to our seats, so she could count heads, and we eventually got our sandwiches.

The next stop was more ominous, with uniformed French soldiers boarding the train to make an announcement: "All able-bodied men and boys needed to deboard and join the Allied Forces in its fight against the Germans. Those from Poland, like my father, would be returned to Poland to join the Polish Army.

Abe in the Polish Cavalry, far right

My heart sank when the officers instructed my father, my cousin Shlomo, and Gusta's fiancé Max to gather their belongings and prepare to leave the train. The three men had no qualms about fighting against the Germans. My father had served in the Polish Cavalry as a young man and was an experienced soldier; he had always fought for justice. But Shlomo and Max were young men who had not yet experienced war or battle.

The French soldiers directed my uncle, Hersh, to also leave the train, sending his wife, Esther, to her knees. Suddenly, she began to sob, pleading with the men not to take her husband, as we needed a male head of family to keep us together. With so many young children in our party, the soldiers took pity on her– and us–and let my uncle remain on board with the promise that he would enlist as soon as we reached our destination and settled in.

I cried bitterly as my father was led from the train. Before deboarding, he handed my mother all the money he had in his pockets, about twenty thousand Belgian francs and 1,500 American dollars. He, like many European Jews, had long feared that something like this might happen and had been saving in case we had to suddenly go on the run.

Antisemitism had been on the rise in Germany since the early 1930s, so he, like other Jewish families, had quietly prepared for what seemed an inevitability. He and my mother created an emergency fund, setting aside cash on a regular basis. They even managed to stash away American dollars–the most stable currency available.

It was a relief to have my father's emergency fund. But it was difficult to think of all that we had left behind. My father had worked many years to build his tailoring business, and suddenly it was gone, as was my mother's treasured silverware and her custom-made clothing.

The train ride to Caraman without my father seemed to take forever. The episode with the French soldiers had frightened everyone, but we tried to console each together as best we could. Much of the journey was fraught with danger; the Germans were bombing the railroad lines, forcing the engineer to continually change direction. For a time, we'd be traveling in a car at the front of the train. But then there'd be a bombing, and the train would reverse direction, placing us in the rear car. On and on we moved; no one knew when or if we would ultimately reach our destination.

We spent five days and nights on that train. We were now a party of eleven, and all of us were refugees.

I sometimes wonder how I was able to deal with all this turmoil. I was so young, and my whole world was changing before me. New faces, new places, and my father was now gone. He had always been there for me. To this day, I can vividly remember how scared I felt when he was pulled from the train, and my mother and I were suddenly on our own.

TWO

Gisa and Abraham

What I didn't know until I decided to write this book is that both of my parents had endured great turmoil and loss as children. Both were born in Poland, and both lost one of their parents at a young age.

My mother, Gisa Jassem, was born on August 1, 1912, in Lancut, a small town in southeastern Poland known for its Renaissance castle. Gisa was the youngest child born to Chaim Joseph Jassem and Golda (nee Gottdank) Jassem. She had six siblings: four brothers, Elimelech, Zanvil, Hersch, and Zalmon, and two sisters, Chaya and Malka, whom everyone called Mitsche.

My grandfather, Chaim, was a butcher. He made a decent living, and the family was always well cared for. He was an Orthodox Jew and had his own shop in the center of town, not far from the magnificent Lancut Castle–one of the most beautiful residences in all of Poland. Dating back to the 1600s, the castle was built by Grand Marshall of the Crown Stanislaw Lubomirski, a Polish nobleman who employed a Jewish property manager to care for the stately residence. It was around this time that Jews began to settle in Lancut, and for centuries they were safe and protected by the owners of the castle.

Chaim Yosef Jassem with family.

During World War I, when the property was owned by the Potocki family, Count Potocki employed a handful of Jewish people, declaring they were necessary to run the castle. According to family lore, my great aunt supplied some of the meat for the castle, and it was my great uncle who made the deliveries. It was rumored that Count Potocki's brother had married a Jewish woman, so he was protective of her family, and in turn, the Jews of Lancut.

My mother was six years old in 1918 when her mother, Golda (for whom I am named), developed a throat infection that landed her in the hospital. Unfortunately, there were no antibiotics to cure her, and she soon died from her illness. She was just forty-two years old when she passed. Her death placed a tremendous burden on her eldest daughter, Malka, who was just thirteen at the time and had to step into her mother's shoes.

My grandfather Chaim was strict, and he had high expectations for his children. Every evening, he would check that all of their shoes were polished and that the house was clean. He was an early riser, and in the mornings, he would take a shot of Slivovitz–a fruit brandy made from damson plums–to get his blood flowing. He was a good father, an Orthodox Jewish man who believed in religion and education, and he tried to manage the best he could. When he had extra income, he hired tutors so his children could learn foreign languages. He never wanted to remarry because he was fearful that any woman he brought into the house might not treat his children well.

In 1920, two years after Golda's death, Chaim sent my mother to live with relatives in Berlin, some 500 miles away. Worried that there was no future for his youngest child in Lancut, he somehow managed to have her smuggled into Germany on a train accompanied by a cousin. She was just eight years old at the time.

Gisa suffered in Berlin during those early years. Being so far from home, she was lonely without her brothers and sisters. The cousins she had been sent to live with did not especially want her there; she was a burden, and they made that clear in the way she was treated.

Life brightened when Gisa's older brother, Zalmon, and his wife, who was also named Gisa, invited her to come and live with them and their young son, Max, in their cozy flat in Berlin. The young family had recently left Poland for Germany in hopes of finding financial stability.

It was Zalmon's wife, Gisa, who taught my mother to cook, sew, and keep house, and it was under Gisa's tutelage that she learned how to become a seamstress, a skill that would eventually enable her to earn a living.

Zalmon and Gisa (his wife) in Berlin.

For a short time, my mother's older sisters, Chaya and Mitsche, came to Berlin, where Zalmon's wife taught them to sew, so they, too, could support themselves as seamstresses when they returned home to Poland. Remarkably, I still have an old black and white photo of the three sisters posing in the dresses they surely made themselves.

My mother only attended school until the age of thirteen, but she was well-read. In her free time, she frequented the library in Berlin, and many years later, when I was born, she shared her love of books with me.

The year my mother turned thirteen, tragedy befell the family. Little Max, who was now five, got appendicitis. Sadly, doctors did not diagnose the condition in time, and his appendix ruptured. An infection set in and spread quickly through his body, causing his organs to fail and ultimately killing him.

It was a difficult time for everyone. Zalmon and Gisa went on to have two daughters, Gerda (Zahava) and Hilla (Yael), but Max remained a cherished memory.

In Berlin, my mother became a real urbanite. She loved going to movies, the theater, and museums. She joined the Jewish Scouts, too, and became enthralled with gymnastics, a pursuit she would continue well into adulthood. She especially loved walking for exercise and kept it up almost to the end of her life. She cared about fashion and preferred wearing high heels, even when she was out on one of her regular walks. Even in her older years, she had a hard time giving up her cherished high heels. The reality was that Gisa loved being a Berliner–but that would soon change. Adolph Hitler's rise to power dampened her love for the bustling city.

Gisa and friends at Berlin ball, 1928.

As Hitler's influence grew, the political climate in Germany became hostile, and there were growing outbreaks of violence against Jews. The Gestapo, the Nazis, and the "Brownshirts"–a violent paramilitary group that supported Hitler–made it uncomfortable for my mother to be out on the streets.

On one evening walk, Gisa, now twenty-one, was followed for miles by a man in uniform. No longer feeling safe out on the streets alone, she arranged to visit her brother Hersh, who had left Lancut and was now living in Belgium with his wife, Esther, and their eight children.

Zalmon came home one evening to find his baby sister packing her suitcase and asked what she was doing.

Gisa told him about the frightening incident with the German soldier and how she no longer felt safe in Berlin. Her plan was to travel across the border to Belgium, where she would stay with their brother, Hersh, and his family in Liege.

Like a good "father," Zalmon gave her his blessing and some money to tide her over and wished her safe passage. That evening, Gisa left Germany.

In Liege, Hersh owned a butcher shop. Behind the store was a small, two-bedroom apartment where the family lived. All the children shared one bedroom; the boys slept in one bed and the girls in another, all head to foot, or *"tsefeisens."*

Gisa's passport photo.

Hersch in butcher shop, Belgium.

Despite the tight quarters, Gisa was happy in Liege. She found comfort in the city's small Jewish community. It was a close-knit one, and everyone knew one another. It was here that she met her soon-to-be husband, Abraham Miller.

Like Gisa, Abraham also hailed from Poland. He was born on November 28, 1905, in Boleslawiec, a historic town on the Bóbr River about three hours northwest of my mother's hometown of

Lancut. He had an older sister, Zeisel, and two younger brothers, whose names I do not know. His father, Mordechai, was a "businessman" who regularly traveled to Germany with a horse and wagon to buy whatever goods he could find and return to sell in Poland. I guess you could call it a simple import and export business.

Mordechai Miller

Being the eldest son, my father would sometimes accompany his father to Germany, where they would spend a night and eat their meals at a Jewish rooming house. On one such trip, Mordecai's father fell ill and instructed his twelve-year-old son to locate the landlady to ask her for a cup of tea. But when Abraham returned with the tea, he found his father dead, likely the result of a massive heart attack.

Mordecai's passing meant the effective end of the family's small business. Thankfully, he had left his wife, my grandmother, Sprintzer, with enough money to start her own trading business. He had also hidden several gold pieces underground, so that the family would not be penniless.

At twelve years old, Abraham was apprenticed to a men's tailoring atelier. When he came of age, he joined the Polish Army. He was assigned to the cavalry and rose to the rank of corporal, a big feat for a Jewish soldier.

After his service, he decided to leave Poland. He'd heard from a good friend that there were great opportunities for men's tailors in Paris, so he set off for the City of Light, where he hoped to make his fortune. But he had little money, and what he had ran out by the time he reached Belgium. Unable to afford a ticket to Paris, he had no choice but to get off the train and look for a job.

Unfortunately, the only work available was in the coal mines.

Like many of his fellow miners, my father owned just one work outfit–a pair of pants and a jacket. His lack of clothing made things extraordinarily difficult in the mines, where dust and dirt were everywhere. Before descending into the mine, he turned his pants inside out. Then, before going home, he would remove his pants and knock them against a wall to remove the coal dust as best he could.

Eventually, Abraham was able to save enough money to open a small tailoring shop in the city of Seraing, about eight kilometers from Liege. Some of his first customers were the Italians who had worked alongside him in the mines. By the time he met my mother, he was a successful entrepreneur with his own business and apartment.

The two first laid eyes on each other at a local Hanukkah ball. There was just one problem: my mother was on a date with another young man that night, so the two never got a chance to talk. But my father left the dance that evening, determined to learn more about this pretty, Polish woman who had captured his attention.

As fate would have it, the two crossed paths again several days later. My mother had agreed to accompany her brother to a friend's apartment for dinner, and who should be sitting at the kitchen table but Abraham Miller.

Upon seeing Gisa, he immediately excused himself so that he could run home to shave and change his clothes. Abraham was a men's tailor, and he prided himself on being well-dressed.

At the end of the evening, he invited Gisa out on a date and was disappointed when she turned him down. But Abraham was persistent, and, after several more invitations, she agreed to go out with him.

The two had been dating for just a short time, the day a police officer showed up at Hersh's apartment looking for my mother. Abraham was waiting at the kitchen table for my mother to emerge from the bedroom, where she was primping for their evening out, when the officer came knocking. He was there to inform my mother that her visa had expired and she needed to leave Belgium. She had already renewed it three times, and there were no more renewals available to her.

"Who is this?" the officer asked my mother, pointing to the well-dressed man with the black eyes and wavy hair.

"He's my boyfriend," Gisa replied.

The policeman began questioning Abraham, asking about his living arrangements and his profession.

"I live in Seraing, I have a store, I'm a tailor, and my name is Abraham Miller," my father replied.

"Do you like this girl?" the officer inquired, pointing at my mother.

"Yes, of course," Abraham said without hesitation.

"I will come to your home tomorrow," the officer told Abraham. "And if you make a good living and everything is like you say it is, you will marry her, okay?"

My father quickly agreed.

Somehow, the policeman was able to file some paperwork and make the visa issue go away, at least temporarily.

One year later, on March 17, 1933, Abraham and Gisa were married at her brother's house under a *chuppah* before twelve guests. Gisa wore a long, pink dress that my father purchased for her, and the two celebrated with a dinner prepared by Hersh's wife, Esther. The wedding gifts consisted of two pillowcases and a tablecloth.

"Don't worry, you will have everything you will need," Abraham told his bride that day.

He did, indeed, have a nice apartment with a lot of silver things, but it needed a good cleaning because of all the ashes from the coal stove. A year and several months later, I arrived at 1:00 p.m. on July 7, 1935. I was born in the local hospital, where the nurses were nuns.

When they asked for my name, my parents said, "Golda," after my mother's mother. But the nuns cautioned that I might have a problem in school with a name like that–a Jewish name–so my parents changed it to Gilda with a soft "G."

Gilda and Abe on street in Liege, 1937.

We had a good life in Belgium. My father's business thrived, and he was able to open a large atelier. We now lived in Liege in a spacious apartment behind the shop. There was a backyard where I could play, and my parents even got a kitten for me. We had lots of friends.

Cousin Frida with Gilda and kitten.

Every summer, my father would close the shop for several weeks, and we would go on vacation.

Gilda wins 1st prize at costume contest, Liege, 1939.

I was two years old in the summer of 1937 when we traveled to Germany and Poland to visit relatives. Our first stop was Berlin, which I'm sure was scary for my mother. She feared the Germans but wanted to see members of our family who were still there.

Gilda with Gisa and Abe, Liege, 1938 - studio photo.

I got very ill while in Berlin and had to go see *"Herr Professor,"* a well-known doctor. I must not have tolerated the bacteria in the city's water, and I had a bad stomachache. When I recuperated, we traveled to Lancut, Poland, to meet the rest of the Jassem family on my mother's side.

Gilda, age 3.

This was my parents' first trip back to Poland since leaving the country. My father told me there were so many extended family members that it took one week to meet them all and another week to say goodbye.

Abe Miller with Benjamin Miller and family (Lodz, Poland, 1937)

Our next stop was the city of Lodz to meet the Miller family, who had relocated from Boleslawiec. Our first stop was my father's mother's home. My mother looked fashionable in a custom-made dress and hat, complemented by a stone marten fur stole, which mysteriously disappeared during our visit.

Benjamin Miller and family.

When it was time to leave, she searched all over the house and finally found it where it had been secreted away by my aunt Zeisel, who apologized to my mother. Apparently, my aunt had hidden it so that she could keep it and wear it after my parents left. According to my father, his sister Zeisel was envious of my mother, whom she viewed as sophisticated, well-dressed, and very pretty.

This would be our last visit with family in Poland. Two years later, the Germans would invade the country. I was four years old when the invasion happened. My parents had sent me to a sleep-away camp in Blanckenberg, a beach resort in Belgium, along with Esther, my eleven-year-old friend. They had arranged to stay at a hotel about ninety minutes away, where they could enjoy some quiet time together.

I was at the camp for only a few days when my parents showed up to take me home. I was too young to understand what was happening. But my parents were worried. The Nazis had marched into Poland and it wouldn't be long before the bombs would start dropping on Belgium and we would be on a train to France, hoping to stay one step ahead of the invading army.

THREE

Caraman, France

The train ride to Caraman without my father seemed to take forever. Thankfully, the people of Caraman were surprisingly generous. Residents kindly opened their doors to us, and this small town quickly became our home. My mother and I were invited to stay with a local pharmacist and his family. (Unbeknownst to me, I would one day marry a pharmacist.) The family was very kind to us. They treated us well, and we felt welcome in their home.

My uncle, Hersh, was offered a vacant house in the village for his very large family. Other people fleeing the Germans were also taken into homes in the area.

We were more fortunate than some. In Caraman, we had a roof over our heads and a place to sleep. Still, we felt abandoned and desperate. We were lucky that, as Jews, we were able to move about freely. In Germany, the Jewish people were under siege. That past November, the German government issued the "Decree on the Elimination of the Jews from Economic Life," barring Jews from operating stores and from carrying on trade of any kind. Jewish children were banned from attending German public schools. And other atrocities were occurring against the Jewish people that we would only learn of later.

In Caraman, at least, there were no limits placed upon us.

Despite the danger we faced, my mother said she felt like a teenager again, being able to spend time with her nieces and nephews. As the youngest member of the tribe, I was dragged all over the place by my older cousins. During one especially daring (and perhaps risky) adventure, we kids raided a fruit orchard and made off with a cache of peaches and cherries. These risky escapades were a much-needed distraction and likely helped me to deal with the anxiety that I was feeling at being separated from my father.

Meanwhile, the war raged around us. On May 26, the Germans advanced into France, trapping Allied troops on the beaches of Dunkirk. The attack on Dunkirk set in motion the biggest evacuation in military history, with more than 330,000 British and Allied troops evacuated using naval vessels and hundreds of civilian boats.

Thankfully, my parents had "forgotten" the location of the room they had rented for us in Dunkirk. In Caraman, we were safe, at least for the time being. Still, we had no idea how long we would be permitted to stay or how long our money would last.

My uncle Hersh was eager to find a job, but there were few opportunities in the small village. He would need to travel to a city where his prospects would be better. The problem was that we couldn't move from one place to another without permission from French officials. During our short time in Caraman, my uncle had forged a friendship with the mayor and was able to secure a day pass to the nearby city of Toulouse.

Not wanting her brother to travel alone, my mother volunteered to join him. She also had another reason for wanting to go there. Since the war broke out, people fleeing to safety had become separated from loved ones. Or, like my father, they had been taken into the armed forces to fight the Germans. Communication was limited, so people had taken to posting notes and signs around the train stations, asking for information about their missing loved ones.

At four, I had just started to read. I remember seeing dozens of papers posted on the walls of every train station, with people looking for family members. Many included information on where they could be found, with the hope of somehow reuniting with loved ones. My mother wanted to post her messages to my father around the stations in Toulouse, letting my father know where he could find us. Meanwhile, I would stay back in Caraman with my aunt and cousins.

The mayor had only been able to grant my mother and her brother a single day pass, so we waited with anticipation for their return. But by nightfall, they had not yet come back to Caraman. We didn't worry; my mother had told my aunt that if it got too late, she and my uncle would spend the night in Toulouse.

I awoke to the joyous sound of my mother's voice. She and my uncle had good news to share. Hersh had found a job at a butcher shop in one of the markets, and there was information about my father.

In Toulouse, my mother had experienced a miracle. She and my uncle were walking through one of the open-air markets when she spotted Leo Rottenberg, a friend from Liege and the husband of her best friend, Enna. Leo, too, was out looking for work. He and his family had fled Liege the same night that we did and ended up in Toulouse, where he and his wife were lucky enough to find an apartment big enough to accommodate their extended family.

Leo was traveling with his wife Enna, their daughter Fanny, Enna's brother, Karl Gittman, Karl's wife Rika, their daughter Stella, and Karl's parents. Excitedly, Leo pointed out the building in which they were staying.

Remarkably, the Gittmans were the couple who had rented the apartment in Dunkirk, France, with my parents. Now, they were here in Toulouse, safe and sound. Leo even had news about my father. He had learned Abraham was now attached to the Polish Army and was in Bressuire, France, waiting to be deployed to England. It was a relief to know he was okay, but there was no word on my cousin Shlomo, or Gusta's fiancé, Max.

With my uncle Hersh having found a new job and the Rottenbergs' apartment now available, the family's path forward was clear: We could gather up our things and move to Toulouse.

Soon, we were all on the train. But when we arrived at our friends' apartment, we were met with unexpected news: France had surrendered to the Germans and was going to be occupied by Hitler's army. The Gittmans and Rottenbergs would flee immediately and suggested that we do, too. Their plan was to travel to Bayonne, a port city in southwestern France, where they hoped to board a ship for England.

After a lengthy conversation, it was decided that we would go with the group to Bayonne.

The group was taking taxis out of the city, and we, too, got into two taxis and followed them. Luckily, we found drivers who were willing to go far beyond the city limits. One driver told us he would take the family as far as his gasoline would hold out. None of us had any clue as to how much these taxi rides would cost, but we were confident that we would find some way to work things out.

Hersh's eldest daughter, Gusta, had some money from her fiancé, Max, to cover at least part of the expense. As we traveled from one city to the next, we hit one checkpoint after another. At each checkpoint, police asked to see our travel papers. No one was allowed to move from one place to another without the necessary documents. When our parties finally arrived at the French border control point, we were asked for even more papers, which we didn't have. The control point was located in a small town, and so the issue was elevated to the local mayor.

My mother appealed to the mayor for the papers and the permission we needed. She even took the unusual step of asking all of the children to cry, hoping that a bunch of weeping youngsters would convince him to take pity on the group and let us pass. Her ruse worked, and the mayor granted us the right to go to the next town.

The taxi drivers stayed with us until dark. By then, their gasoline tanks were running dry, so they had no choice but to drop us in the quaint Pyrenees town of Luchon and head back. They left with a wad of cash from my mother and Gusta. But we were in an extraordinarily difficult situation, with no place to stay for the night and no way to continue our journey to safety. Somehow, once in Luchon, we became separated from the Gittmans and Rottenbergs. Once again, it was just eleven of us.

With no other choice, my mother decided she would appeal to the mayor one more time. It was dark when she took her niece Lola—another of Hersh's daughters, who was not much younger than my mother—to the mayor's house. There, they knocked on his door and waited, hoping that he would agree to speak to them.

Finally, the mayor came down in his pajamas and asked them what they wanted. My gutsy mother told him a whole story–how we needed to go to the Polish consulate because my father was being sent to England, and his only daughter, me, was crying to see him. She told him that she had no passport and no papers and had nowhere else to go.

At first, the mayor declined to help because, again, we didn't have the correct documentation. But my mother showed him that she had previously obtained permits to go from Toulouse to Luchon. If he could just add Bayonne to the travel documents, we would be able to proceed. She said he need not even add his name to the papers. But he refused. She had no choice but to return to where the rest of the family was waiting in town.

Unwilling to give up, she went to see him one last time, and after much pleading, the mayor relented and gave her the necessary permits.

On the way back, my mother, who was still very young at the age of twenty-seven, ran into another friend from Liege, a woman who had also managed to escape from Belgium. My mother showed her our papers.

"You know you could sell those papers for $2,000," the friend told her.

"Why should I sell them? I need them for my own family," my mother replied.

Her friend said that her husband was also in the army in Bressuire. But he had been discharged and was coming back to Bayonne. She told my mother how he had sent her a postcard, urging her to wait for him.

The woman's story prompted my mother to start wondering about my father's whereabouts. She wondered if he, too, might have been discharged from the army. *If he had indeed been discharged, where could he be?*

Later that evening, my mother and Lola reunited with Hersh and the rest of the family in the town square. The two managed to find an abandoned store and all eleven of us crowded inside, happy to have some place with a roof over our heads. Once we were all safe, my mother and Lola went to the train station to look for soldiers, hoping my father might be among them, but there was no train and no soldiers.

I was too young for my mother to share her fears and concerns with me, but I knew that she missed my father terribly and wanted us to be reunited. She had left a postcard message at the train station in Caraman for my father, hoping that he might come searching for us. She had written on the card that we were in Toulouse. And she'd been sure to tell other friends she'd encountered in Toulouse that we were going to Bayonne. It was a bit like leaving breadcrumbs behind, hoping that my father would pick up on our journey and follow along.

My mother had a strong feeling that she would meet up with him again. Perhaps it was intuition or maybe even extra-sensory perception. *Who knows what pushed her?* But somehow, she had this gut feeling that he would be able to find us.

FOUR

On Route to Bayonne

The following day, we boarded a train, anxious to continue our journey. At one point during the ride, we stopped in St. Croix, where we had to change trains for Bayonne. During the transfer, my mother bumped into a friend's husband, another refugee from Liege. (It is incredible to think of how many refugees from Liege we encountered during this harrowing journey.) My mother ran over, hugged him, and asked if he had seen my father.

"Sure," he said. "When I left Toulouse, he was sleeping in the train station."

My mother asked if my father was with Shlomo and Max at the train station. But the man said that he appeared to be traveling alone.

For reasons that I never understood, my mother had this strong feeling that my father was somewhere on our train, and she told her brother that she believed my father, Shlomo, and Max were now on board.

She had expected they were all in uniforms since they had been in the army, and she believed they were all headed to Bayonne. At each station, she told her nieces to get out and run alongside the train, yelling the names of our relatives, "Abraham!" "Max!" "Shlomo!"

Time and again, the girls called out for them, but no one responded.

I was scared, and I wouldn't let my mother out of my sight. One parent had already been torn from me, and I wasn't going to let my mother go, but it was difficult for her to run with me dragging along. The platforms were crowded, with terrified people trying to flee to safety. Still, I clung to her and cried hysterically.

The next station was bedlam. Thousands of people were milling around, looking for loved ones. Again, the walls were covered with papers, people looking for missing relatives. Years later, my mother recalled that scene, telling me that she'd never seen anything like it.

She still had a very strong feeling that my father and my cousins were on our train. She sent Gusta out once more to scout around the station and see if she could find them. I remember her running up and down the platforms, shouting out their names, but to no avail. Then, by sheer miracle, my father recognized Gusta from the back and shouted her name.

"Papa!" she yelled as she ran toward him. (Everyone called my father "Papa.")

Gusta, now nineteen, jumped into his outstretched arms, and they hugged as their eyes filled with tears.

My mother had been searching for men in uniform, but she'd been wrong. My father was dressed in civilian clothes. We were now reunited, and tears of joy ran down our faces. My mother had mixed emotions. She was overjoyed to have found my father, but saddened that Shlomo and Max were nowhere to be found.

Over time, we would slowly piece together the story of what had happened to my father and nephews. When the three men arrived in Bressuire, the army unit was decommissioned. Some of the men went to England, but my father wanted to stay in France so that he could reunite with the family. The army told the men that they had to find their way back alone, and, at some point in the journey, my father and his nephews became separated.

My father had to walk, hitch a ride, find some way to get back to us. It was many kilometers, and he had to travel most of the way on foot. Fortunately, he was in good physical shape and very strong. It took about three or four days to walk to Caraman, where he found the message from my mother, and then to Toulouse. Then, he learned that we had all left for Bayonne and needed to board the train. Remarkably, we had all been traveling on the very same train that day, though we hadn't caught a glimpse of each other during the journey until my father spotted Gusta searching the platform for him.

We stayed in Bayonne for several days and continued to go back to the train station, looking for Max and Shlomo. First, one appeared and then the other. Finally, we were all reunited.

Miracles do happen. How can you explain that with thousands of people going hither and yon, that we would all find one another and become a whole family of fourteen people once more? Many tears of happiness and gratitude were shed.

Though it was marvelous to have the family together again, we still had practical challenges to confront, including finding a place for all of us to sleep in Bayonne. After searching around for a while, we discovered an empty school building and some hay mattresses. But we soon learned that the Nazis were headed towards the area, and there were fears that the locals would be unable to protect any of the Jewish refugees. The children were provided gas masks by the locals to protect them from the coming onslaught.

It quickly became clear that we had to leave Bayonne, but where could we go? It seemed that we were barely able to stay one or two steps ahead of the Nazis, and our situation was growing increasingly tenuous.

We heard that there were visas to Portugal, Spain, Morocco, and some North African countries available. The North African cities had become a haven for refugees after the signing of the Franco-German Armistice on June 22, 1940. (The armistice agreement divided France into a German-occupied zone and a nominally free Vichy-regime zone, which included French Morocco.)

We needed to leave Bayonne, but we also needed the documentation that would allow us to travel. The family devised a plan for all the adults to go to the various consulates to try to get the necessary papers to leave France. Others suggested that we might be able to depart via ship if we could find suitable accommodation.

My father and Hersh headed for the Moroccan consulate. There, hundreds of men in suits and hats were waiting in line outside the building, but somehow, they pushed their way forward and got inside to speak to one of the officials.

Although my father stood just 5'4", he had the ego of a six-foot man. He never let his size prevent him from getting what he wanted or needed.

My father described how he'd just been discharged from the Polish Army and was trying to find some way to leave France with his large family. He said we would like to go to Casablanca.

The Moroccan officials empathized with his plight and granted him the necessary papers, wishing him luck with the journey. "If you can get a boat, you can go," they were told.

No one knew how to secure a boat for the trip across the Mediterranean. We headed toward Bayonne's waterfront, where we gathered quietly on the pier alongside a cargo ship. My parents and aunt and uncle made a joke that somehow a boat would magically appear and take us all to Casablanca. But in their hearts, they knew that was all but impossible. Still, everyone kept a positive outlook, even faced with such dire circumstances. After all, despite all odds, we had somehow all been reunited. We just needed to stay together and believe in good fortune.

Soon, other refugees joined us on the pier, and it wasn't all that long before there were hundreds of us waiting, hoping for some possibility of transport. With every passing hour, more people showed up. Perhaps there were 400 or 500 of us there waiting, hoping for safe passage.

All the noise prompted the captain of the cargo ship docked in the harbor to walk out onto the deck and stare down at all of us waiting on the pier. His name was Captain Snow, and he asked why we were all standing there.

Some of those in the crowd shouted that we needed transportation to Casablanca. But the captain said he couldn't help, because he was hauling a cargo of bananas to England.

Some on the pier were Communists who had escaped from the Spanish Civil War. They, too, were now in danger and looking for a safe haven. There was no indication from the captain that he would change his mind, and so we had no choice but to continue to wait, hoping for a miracle.

Things took a turn for the worse as it started to rain. The conditions were miserable for all of us—for the old and infirm and the young children. One of the refugees was carrying a baby that was just eight days old. There was no food and nothing to drink, either.

My uncle and some others went in search of food. They found a shop where they bought cheese and bread and whatever would not spoil and carried it back to the pier in burlap bags. Soon, everything was wet, as the rain continued to pour down on the bedraggled and frightened crowd.

Some of the foodstuffs were almost inedible, but there was nothing we could do, and we dared not throw anything away, as we had no idea when we might get something else to eat.

No doubt, the captain had been watching the scene from his perch high overhead on the ship. Taking pity on us, he told the crowd that he would try to do something for us the next day–but that we must leave and then return to the pier when the time was right. But we had nowhere to go, and we also had no idea when the Nazis might march into Bayonne.

Could we go back to the abandoned school with the hay mattresses?

Now, there were about 500 of us, not just the fourteen members of my family. The captain apparently tried speaking to his superiors, hoping to be able to provide shelter for us on the boat. But there was nothing he could do, at least not right away.

Then people started to sing "La Marseillaise," the French National Anthem. I was young, but I remember that moment like it was yesterday. We could see that Captain Snow was very touched by the whole scene. Soon, he, himself, cried along with us.

He had such empathy that he made a deal with us. The captain promised to take us as far as he could, which was Portugal. But we would have to feed ourselves and sleep wherever there was space on board. And, to make room for all of us amid the crew, he would have to throw the cargo of bananas overboard. We were warned not to eat them; they were green and would cause illness if eaten.

That afternoon, my family found refuge from the rain in a gazebo in the center of town. My mother changed my clothes into dry ones. She had been wearing a crepe de chine dress, but it was soaking wet and miserable. She ripped some of the fabric away, which shortened the garment to a mini dress, which was not fashionable in those days; her fur wraps barely covered her.

That night, we went back to the schoolhouse, where most of the refugees spent a second night–some on hay mattresses and others sleeping on the floor.

Outside, the rain continued to pour. The contents of the burlap bags, the wet bread, cheese, salami, and sausages, were all that we had to eat.

Early the next morning, my uncle went to the pier and saw that smoke was coming out of the ship's smokestacks. He felt encouraged that we might actually be able to leave and quickly ran back to the schoolhouse.

"Children, get up, there is smoke coming out of the smokestacks, and we will be rescued," he excitedly said in Yiddish.

When we returned to the ship, we found that Captain Snow, who was such a decent person, had taken in some old people and given them his cabin, so that they would not have to suffer anymore.

As we boarded the ship, people started to push.

"You don't have to push," he said. "Everyone will be able to get on without a problem."

The men and crew made good on their promise to throw the ship's cargo of bananas over the side to make room for its new cargo of refugees. Green bananas and more green bananas were everywhere, but none that we could eat.

It was after we all got on board that Captain Snow explained what he'd been trying to do for us. He told us how he had first tried to arrange something with the shipping company, but they refused to do anything. Amazingly, he had taken it upon himself to take all of us to Portugal. Unfortunately, there was nowhere near enough food in the ship's supplies to be able to feed the hundreds who were coming aboard. But at least we could get out of Bayonne alive, and that meant the world to us.

Looking back on that day, I now realize that the captain was putting himself at great risk, first by disposing of the green banana cargo and then by ferrying all of us to Portugal.

My father and the other adults brought all the burlap bags full of food onboard. The bags were all thoroughly soaked, and some of the food, especially the bread, was inedible. But at least we were all on board, and food seemed like a secondary issue. We were just so happy to be able to escape.

All of us remained on that cargo ship for eight days as it slowly sailed to Portugal. The captain agreed to share whatever food he had on board for the crew with the rest of us. There wasn't nearly enough, but it was something. The food was good, but so many were seasick, especially my mother and I, that we couldn't eat anything anyway.

The captain feared going too far offshore with his precious cargo of refugees, as he had nowhere near enough lifeboats or life jackets, so he sailed just a few miles off the Spanish coast. During the eight days aboard, most of us slept on the hard steel decks. We didn't change clothes for many days and couldn't wash, so you can imagine, after throwing up and not washing, how we must have reeked.

Finally, we reached a port in Portugal, and the captain told us he was going ashore to try to obtain help from a Jewish agency there.

None of us could get off the ship because we didn't have the necessary papers. Documents granting my family passage to Morocco were of no value in Portugal.

Astonishingly, we soon learned that the captain had secured passage for all of us on another ship bound for Morocco. He said he had arranged everyone to "sail first class," which meant that we would be provided the largest and most comfortable accommodations on board. We would also have the best food.

"You've suffered enough," the captain told us.

As a "thank you" gift for all his kindness, the refugees wanted to collect money to give to him, but Captain Snow refused. "If you want to give a gift, give it to poor people," he said. "I don't need it."

Captain Snow was French and truly very kind. He told us that he couldn't live with the thought of leaving all these refugees for the Nazis. A book was eventually published telling of these events. Sadly, on a subsequent trip, the good Captain Snow's ship was hit by a torpedo fired from a German ship, and he was killed on his way to England. His bravery is a thing to be admired and remembered. He put his own safety at risk to save others.

We stayed in port for a few days but never set foot on Portuguese land. We transferred directly from one ship to another using lifeboats. Our voyage from Portugal to Morocco was a welcome respite from the very difficult conditions that we had endured on Captain Snow's cargo ship.

This second ship was large, and every couple got their own cabin, where people could have privacy, collect their thoughts, and wash and change their clothes. We spent several days on board that ship, which was more than enough time for everyone to wash up, clean their garments, and relax a bit. The food wasn't so abundant, but nevertheless, there was enough to eat.

Most of the crew were Haitian, so we managed to communicate with them in French. My father became friendly with them and brought the best food for us. Unfortunately, there was not much he could do for my mother, who continued to be seasick during that trip. Any time she tried to eat anything, she vomited. She would continue to suffer from motion sickness for many years until the drug Dramamine was discovered.

FIVE

Sunny Casablanca

Sunny Casablanca! That was our final port. Upon landing in the North African city, we went through Customs, where our luggage was searched. We had to declare what money we had, and everything had to be legal.

My parents still had most of the 20,000 francs and the $1,500 they started out with, and they were required to deposit it into a bank account in Morocco. Once we were processed, we were loaded into vans and taken to a refugee camp called "Einshuk," which was just outside the city.

Einshuk had once been a jail for Arabs, but now it housed hundreds of refugees. We slept in tents, ate communal style, and bathed in tents. We became a large community of refugees. We hung out together, played together, and tried to make a semblance of life, while the Jewish agency, HIAS–the world's oldest refugee agency–worked to place us in different homes. Little by little, people left the camp. We were there, however, for two weeks.

Children in Einshuk refugee camp, 1940.

Each day, my father would go into the city to look for work. Being a men's tailor, he was soon employed. We rented a room in the French Quarter on the top floor of a building. I guess you would call it a penthouse today. And once again, I adjusted to a new situation and a new place to live.

I liked to climb the stairs to our room, then march around singing French songs that I learned in school, like "Le Petite Soldats" (*little soldiers*). I'd hold a piece of wood and make believe it was a rifle. I still remember some of the songs.

My claim to fame is that I went to kindergarten in Casablanca! And yes, I had a boyfriend, too. I still have a photograph of him. Good looker!

I remember playing outside in the sand-covered playground. I learned how to read and write at a very early age. I even remember getting the Chicken Pox. I still have a pockmark to show for it.

Some of the smells of the *souk* (native market) often come back to haunt me. The scent of rich grains, hummus, and couscous. In my adult travels, I would come upon these familiar smells while visiting other marketplaces, and they would instantly bring me back to Casablanca. Over the years, I've spent a lot of time cooking couscous, trying to recreate those tastes.

To our astonishment, we again found the Gittmans and the Rottenbergs in Morocco. They had settled in Mogador, a town to the south of Casablanca. To our surprise, they, too, had boarded a boat in Bayonne and arrived in Casablanca the very same day that we did. It was yet another miracle.

Gitman family in Casablanca, 1940.

With eight children and Gusta's fiancé, Max, my Uncle Hersh and Aunt Esther needed a larger place than us; so, they had to look outside the city. They ended up in a town called Safi.

Together, we all went to look at their big, old house in the suburbs. My father, Uncle Hersh, a few cousins, and I went inside to check it out. To our great surprise, we happened to see a field mouse, and I let out a screech.

My father thought he was being funny when he grabbed a stick, killed the mouse, then handed it to me by the tail and told me to run outside and bring it to my mother. *Can you imagine the screaming that went on? What did I know?* My father loved to pull jokes of one sort or another with my mom.

Uncle Hersh–who, like his father and brother, had always been a butcher–changed his profession while in Morocco. Instead of butchering, he became a furrier. Just the other side of the animal skin.

It would get cold in the evenings in this desert city, so there was a market for inexpensive fur jackets and coats. After some time, he even employed several people and became somewhat successful. Where before he was always penniless, he now had a thriving business. And, after the war, when he returned to Belgium, he continued to make fur coats and jackets and was able to make a decent living.

Life in Casablanca took on a routine. My dad worked, I went to school, and my mom took care of our home. Whenever they could, my parents spent many hours at the beach on the Mediterranean with their friends and family, enjoying their freedom. Often, they would go to cafés to have pastries and coffee.

My mother told me that it was one of the best times she and my father had. They had no real responsibilities, just work and play. But there was always the fear that the war could come to North Africa. Casablanca was just across the Mediterranean.

The Gittmans had received affidavits from their family in the U.S. that would allow them to emigrate to America. My mother decided she would become their spokesperson and go to the consulate to show their papers. The family was German and had poor knowledge of the French language. My mother was proficient in both German and French, so she volunteered to go with them to speak on their behalf.

It had taken six months for the Gittman family to get an appointment to see the consulate. They had to wait for long hours at his office. Many such refugees were waiting with the same purpose. But they finally got their turn.

My mother, using all her charm and guile, explained the situation and showed the papers on behalf of the Gittman family. She told the consulate that the elder Mrs. Gittman had two sisters and a brother living in New Jersey, and they had sent strong affidavits and now needed visas to travel to America. They had already been denied twice before. Apparently, their affidavit had not been strong enough.

After presenting their case, the Gittmans turned to leave. But my mother remained. Taking a deep breath, she approached the consul to speak on her own behalf. She asked if perhaps she could get visas for herself and her husband and child.

The consul was taken aback by her request. What gall!

Having no proper papers, her arguments had to be very persuasive. He asked her how they would be able to support themselves, as they had no money to live on.

Her response was very forthright. "My husband and I are young, strong, and willing to work hard to support ourselves," she argued.

My mother was a very attractive woman, and I'm sure that didn't hurt her chances any. She pleaded with him; she was forthright, not sassy–just wanting to save her family.

The consul was so impressed with her gutsiness that he told her to bring her husband back to meet him. She agreed but told him that getting an appointment to return would likely take six months, as it had for the Gittmans.

He told her not to worry, he would tell his secretary to let her come the next day, and so, he granted her a visit the very next morning.

She knew her next hurdle would be to send a telegram to Germany to get a quota number as a Polish citizen, because Poland was occupied. That was the regulation then; everything had to come through Germany. My mother was nervous about this and asked the consul if this was really necessary.

"No," he replied. "Don't worry, just forget about it." He was struck by her and made it easier to get the visa.

When she returned with my father the following day, he told her that she was approved. What jubilation she felt! But she was only able to get visas for the three of us. She hoped to be able to send an affidavit for Uncle Hersh and his family once we got to America.

Now, how to get to America?

SIX

Coming to America

Getting transportation to America was another task to conquer. What pushed my mother to want to leave Casablanca so badly was unclear. My father didn't have that same desire; he would have stayed in Morocco for the duration of the war.

But my mother remained unsettled. Perhaps she was concerned about our safety as Jews. America was considered a safe haven, far away from the war raging across Europe.

Twice every day, she went to the boat company, but no luck. Our visa was set to expire on August 1st, my mother's birthday. Then, any new papers would have to come from Washington, D.C. She realized that this would be a last-ditch effort. If she couldn't get immediate passage on a boat, it would be all over.

The agent in charge of approving the travel arrangements was a man named Mr. Castro, and each day my mother would head to the pier in hopes of finding three berths for us to sail on. She went each morning, and he made her come back in the afternoon. Apparently, he liked seeing her. Not only did he have her return daily, but he also wanted to charge her $500 per ticket. That would have been difficult for our family. (People made a lot of money on the misery of others.) Since her need was so strong, she knew that she had to continue to return to the office every day.

While waiting on the pier for a ship to arrive, all the refugees banded around and shared their stories. One day, they were gathered in a nearby café when a rumor began to circulate that a boat sponsored by the Jewish Agency was arriving from Portugal on August 1st, the day our visit was set to expire.

My mother immediately ran home to alert my father, "I'm going to try to get us on this boat."

This was our last chance. My mother felt that in Europe, a woman had a better chance of getting something from a man, so she would be the one to once again approach Mr. Castro.

That afternoon, she returned to the shipping agency and asked to speak to him.

"I've been coming every day for two months and nothing has happened," she told him.

"How much money do you have?" he asked.

"I have $1,100, and that's all we have."

Mr. Castro told her that this would not be enough. "We charge $1,000 per ticket, but come tomorrow at one o'clock."

My mother knew that the offices were closed for lunch at that time, and she said as much.

"Come anyway," Mr. Castro told her. "We will talk it over."

My mother was suspicious of his intentions, and that night she shared her concern with my father. "I know what he wants, I don't trust him," she said.

My parents' family friends, Leo and Enna Rottenberg, were now staying with us in Casablanca while they were trying to obtain their own visas. We all slept in the same room; the Rottenbergs on one side and my parents and I on the other. People made do in such circumstances. Privacy was a luxury that no one could afford. Their daughter Fanny stayed in Mogador with her grandparents.

My mother suggested that Leo and my father accompany her to Mr. Castro's office and wait outside the building while she went inside to meet with him, just in case she ran into trouble.

Sure enough, minutes after arriving, Mr. Castro began lowering the window shades. But my mother wasn't afraid, knowing that Leo and my father were right outside. Taking a seat on the couch, she listened as Mr. Castro invited her to dinner that evening.

When she declined, he got right to the point. "You know, you could have free passage for the three of you," he said.

"How?" she replied, incredulous.

"I will introduce you to the ambassadors; there are the Spanish, French, and Portuguese ambassadors. You come with me, and you'll have a good time."

My mother was silent.

"You aren't the only woman to do this," he continued. "You'll see, you won't have to pay one cent for the boat."

My mother told him she was not interested in this arrangement. "I will not be unfaithful to my husband."

Taking a seat on the couch next to her, Mr. Castro pressed his body close to hers. Uncomfortable, she rose to her feet and said, "I'm not like other women. I must do what I think is right for me."

Her indignation did not change Mr. Castro's mind. Once he saw that she wasn't budging, he told her she needed to go to the Jewish Agency for further help. "I only have a certain number of tickets, and *they* have the rest," he said. "Go to them and perhaps they will do what you want."

The following morning, my mother was up with the sun. By 7:00 a.m. sharp, she was outside the agency's front door, determined to speak to Madam Bernadette, the woman in charge. Sadly, Madam Bernadette was unkind, "a witch," according to my mother, coldly unsympathetic to her plight.

By now, my mother was at her wits' end. She had gotten this far and was determined not to lose this final opportunity to leave for

America. But time was running out. The boat was departing the very next day.

She barely got a chance to tell Madam Bernadette of our plight when the woman cut her off mid-sentence. "I have an appointment, and I don't care if you leave here or not," she barked, causing my mother to cry.

She had been holding herself together throughout the ordeal, but the callousness of this woman cut her like a knife.

Perhaps my mother's tears softened Madam Bernadette, because she suddenly turned back, looked at my mother, and said, "Go to the dock tomorrow morning. There will be a list of passengers, and if your name is on it, you will be able to leave."

The following morning, my mother went to the pier with her friend Enna Rottenberg. Once at the docks, she checked the passenger list and found to her consternation that our names were not on it. She was so upset, and she quickly ran over to Mr. Castro's office. She found him and fell on him like he was a long-lost relative, then burst into tears.

He asked her why she was crying, and she told him that our names were not on the passenger list.

"Madame Bernadette, didn't give you the tickets? Some nerve," he said. "See, if you had slept with me, you'd have gotten the tickets and for free."

"I would like to ask you one question," my mother began. "You're married? You have children, right?"

"Yes," was his response.

"Would you like it if your wife slept with other men? So why should I do it? I can't do that to my husband."

That was the only thing she asked him, and that did it. He then called Madam Bernadette and said she had to give my mother the three tickets for us to get onto the boat.

My mother was a force to be reckoned with. That was how we got to sail on the SS New Guinea; it was really a very close call.

The ship was scheduled to leave in several hours, so my mother had to run home to pack. There wasn't much to take; we had very few possessions at that time. She paid $1,000 for our tickets, which left us with just $220, not a lot of money. She promptly loaned $200 to her best friend Enna, who promised she would give it back once in New York.

Gilda's passport photo, 1941.

Our ship was far from a cruise ship. The SS New Guinea was a converted cargo ship. There were a few cabins for the few women and children. The men slept on bunk beds in the hold, with only the cargo opening for fresh air.

My mother took one whiff of the other ladies' perfumes in the cabin and immediately got seasick. She quickly asked to move. There were no other accommodations, but she promptly announced to the captain that she and I would sleep in the hold with the men.

"Oh my God!" is what the captain must have said or thought. *What to do?*

He told her that she would be embarrassed sleeping there with all those men.

"I'll put up a curtain, and I won't look," was her reply.

So it was that my mother, my father, and I crossed the Atlantic with about 200 men around us. My mother was the worst sailor; just smelling the engine made her violently seasick.

At one point during the journey, I recall standing on some sort of platform–perhaps one of the bunk beds–and singing to entertain everyone. These men were lonely for their families, and I gave them some diversion. I sang all the songs I learned in school. I was not a shy youngster. I like to think I inherited my mother's gutsiness.

Remarkably, some of these men remembered my performance years later when they encountered my father on the streets in New York City and asked if I had gone to Hollywood to become a star. Not so!

The Brooklyn Bridge. 1992 oil painting by the author, Gilda Zirinsky.

We finally arrived not at the closed Ellis Island but at a pier in Brooklyn. The first thing we saw after docking was a man selling Mello Rolls, a t-shaped ice cream cone. *Remember those?* A huge portion. Only a nickel. My father was amazed. He always talked about them.

We landed in New York with just $20 in our pockets. But thanks to my mother, we had arrived. When she got off the boat, she knelt and kissed the ground. She was glad of two things—one, that they were safe, the other that she could finally get off the boat and onto land.

SEVEN

A New Land

We were in a new land, with no money and no place to live. The Hebrew Immigrant Aid Society (HIAS) came to our rescue. They helped all new Jewish immigrants settle. They promised to help people get employment and places to live.

They had a building in lower Manhattan, where they housed incoming refugees. Those seeking help were allowed to remain on their premises for six weeks, free of charge. They often relocated people to parts of the country that were begging for workers. One family we befriended was sent to Cleveland, Ohio. My mother pleaded to remain in New York.

The HIAS premises were also a meeting place for displaced people. My parents became acquainted with other Belgian Jews with whom we would later share living quarters. It was a respite for us all, a safe haven. When you are a refugee, you are not so fussy; you are happy to get whatever you can to make your life better.

I vaguely recall playing with other children and starting my "normal" childhood life once more. I believe HIAS provided English classes since most of us did not speak the language.

Once more, I had to adapt to a whole new situation. As difficult as it was, I am certain that my experiences as a child helped me later in life when I faced my own unexpected and difficult situations.

Eventually, both of my parents found jobs in a coat factory where they manufactured coats for the Army. Ironically, it was in Long Island City, where my future second husband's family would own many properties.

At HIAS, we met up with several people whom we had met in Casablanca, among them the Lindenbergs. Together with them, we rented an attic apartment in Manhattan on 100th Street between Columbus Avenue and Central Park West. Our landlord, a Polish lady, was not very nice, taking advantage of refugees with very few resources. My mother disliked her very much.

Our apartment, again, was very tight quarters, but we were now living in New York City. So, for the moment, my mother was happy. We lasted there for six months, and then we all moved to a larger apartment one block north on 101st Street and Manhattan Avenue, which we again shared with the Lindenbergs. This apartment had two front rooms, I guess they were the two bedrooms, and a kitchen.

My parents and I lived in the living room/dining room part of the apartment. I slept on a cot, my parents on a trundle bed that my mother covered to look like a day bed.

My mother finally enrolled me at school. I'm not sure how she was able to communicate without English, but her classes at HIAS helped her to communicate.

I should have been in the first grade, but I was placed in kindergarten because I didn't speak English. Several weeks later, however, they moved me up to first grade since I had already learned how to read in French, they then promptly moved me to the second grade.

The Lindenberg's daughter, Louise, whom we all called Bijou, meaning "jewel" in French, walked me to and from school each day. She was several years older than I, but we attended the same school.

I remember one time, when I got a piece of dirt in my eye while my mother was at work. Mrs. Lindenberg was at home and called me into the kitchen.

"Look me in the eyes!" she instructed, then she just spat into my eye.

I will never forget that incident. She did, however, get the dirt out of my eye.

I made a new friend in the apartment building who was of Norwegian descent. I don't remember her name, but she invited me for dinner one night. I recall eating broccoli for the first time and still remember the taste. It was a different taste for me. I felt that it was the beginning of my assimilation into our new culture.

My new friend then lent me her Mickey Mouse watch overnight. Curious to see what made it tick, I opened it up, took it apart, and was never able to put it back together. I still remember the guilt. I can't recall what happened after that, since I conveniently blocked it out.

During that same period, I got the mumps. My mother tried to keep me warm and comfortable. She was concerned that I would not keep the covers on while in bed, so she slept with me. *Guess what?* She caught the mumps, too. Only she couldn't take off from work, so she tied her face up with a scarf and told everyone she had a toothache. I guess my mumps must have traveled far and wide in the factory.

Soon, my parents met up with a whole contingent of other Belgian refugees living in the same neighborhood, and our lives took on a new direction. My mother hated working in a factory, so she found a job as a private seamstress nearby.

"I was never meant to work in a factory," was her lament. She didn't mind working, but just not under those circumstances. She hated to hear the other women gripe about their plights. She was so happy to be here in America, and she couldn't understand their complaints.

One day, while still at the factory, she could no longer control her anger and she yelled to them, "If you don't like it here, go back to where you came from!"

Thus was our beginning in the New World.

The Miller and Silverman families at the Statue of Liberty, 1944.

Together with our newfound Belgian friends, our family developed an extensive social circle. These new friends became our substitute family, filling the emptiness caused by a lack of family ties.

Not only were the adults close, but the children were too. There were the Lindenbergs, the Kranzs, the Silvermans, the Fischoffs, and the Mejanagoras (who later moved to California after changing their name to Mego). All the children played together.

Farther west towards Riverside Drive were the Gittmans–Rika, Karl, and Stella–the Schiffs, the Wolfs, and the Rottenbergs. Most of my parents' friends were "shomer shabbos" (Sabbath observers), modern Orthodox Jews, but my parents were not.

I began my education in the public schools, but changed in the second grade to a Yeshiva, a Hebrew day school, along with Fanny and Rachel Kranz and Nathan Silverman. By now, my parents and their friends had a steady income, so they decided that we should attend Yeshiva Soloveitchik in Washington Heights, a private school. Every day, we kids would travel there by subway. Our parents had to work and had no resources to help care for us. Since we were a group, we didn't feel alone.

I was in the second grade in English studies, but since I did not speak or read any Hebrew, they put me back to the first grade–again! Back and forth; back and forth. I'm sure all of this must have been very confusing for me. I had no choice and took it all in stride. I cannot say that I didn't do my share of mischief, but for the most part, I proved to be a model child. I did not want to make waves.

Here we were, four little *pishers* (Yiddish for "little kids"), seven years old, except for Rachel, who was six, traveling alone on the subway day in and day out. We'd get five-cent coupons from the Board of Education, which we traded in for a nickel to put into the turnstile. But now and then, one of us would sneak under the turnstile, cash in the extra coupon, and buy candy, usually a Baby Ruth bar.

We had all arrived in this country within a year of each other and had banded together as a family. Our new friends had come to America from Antwerp, Belgium, some via Cuba, while we came via France and Morocco from Liege, Belgium.

After a year in America, we finally got our own apartment at 50 Manhattan Avenue. It was our own, but very small. It was a studio apartment, no bedrooms. You entered into a large foyer where we first kept a dining room table against the wall and later an upright piano. There was a sleep sofa from Castro Convertibles–from their original showroom on 22nd Street–and two club chairs.

From the foyer, you went down a short hallway to a galley kitchen, and at the end of the kitchen, there was a dinette where my parents kept a small metal table and four chairs. That was where I slept.

My bed was a folding cot that I had to open and close every morning and evening. I had the bottom half of a closet for my belongings, and the top half was the linen closet, and that was it. My parents shared the other closet. I was allowed to keep my toys and such on the floor of my half closet. If I didn't keep them neatly, my mother would threaten to throw them out. I had to run to the incinerator in the hallway many a time to retrieve my belongings. I learned to be neat or else. I guess having such tight quarters, that's the only way to live.

In front of our bathroom was a niche where my mother kept an old Singer sewing machine with a foot treadle that she got from a cousin who lived in Brooklyn. My mother made all my clothes on this machine, and sometimes my father sewed clothes for us on it, too. We were always well-dressed. I learned how to use the sewing machine at an early age and sewed all my doll's clothing.

We remained in the studio apartment on Manhattan Avenue for seven years and managed to survive. It was wartime, and housing was at a premium, so we had no other choice. There was nothing luxurious about our living quarters, but they were modern for the time, and we were safe.

Gilda with Gisa and Abe, New York, 1941 - study photograph.

EIGHT

Newfound Family in America

As it turned out, we did have family here in the United States. My mother had several first cousins from her mother's side who came long before Europe was at war. These cousins had come from Poland. I'm not exactly sure where from.

There was Izzy Stutzel, whom I later called Uncle Izzy, his wife Gussie, and their three children, Bernie, who was married to Alice, Blanche (Bebi), and Seymour. Izzy had a brother, whose name escapes me, and was married to a woman named Tessie. Together, they had two daughters.

There was another cousin, Abe Gottdank, who was married to Sadie and had four children. They all lived in Bensonhurst, Brooklyn. They had arrived many years before us, and all worked in the garment industry. One was a buttonhole maker, one a presser, and so on. All these cousins were relatives of my deceased grandmother, Golda.

Golda Jassem, date unknown.

I was too young to really be curious about their jobs. I just remember going to Brooklyn to visit them frequently. We took the F train to the last stop, Church Avenue, and then a trolley car to their house. It seemed like an endless trip. When we arrived, there were always chicken sandwiches made on Challah dripping with *schmaltz* (chicken fat) waiting for us.

Uncle Izzy loved to spend time with me and taught me how to play cards. We played War, and I would often beat him. I wonder how many times he made himself lose.

Blanche would play the piano; I would sing, and everyone would applaud. She often said, "Here's a little child of only six years old, and she can speak French, and me, a grown woman in her twenties, can't utter a word in that language."

I became the mascot of the household. On our return trips back to Manhattan, my parents bought the *Sunday Daily News*. I would read the comics and promptly fall asleep. I could never stay up late in those years, and I still don't like to.

Occasionally, we would go to Cousin Abe's house, where Sadie would always serve her famous stuffed cabbage. She was always crocheting something or another, her hands were always busy. She was a wee bit of a woman, but always on the move. They had four children, but by then, they had all married and had left home. I only got to know one daughter, Florrie, and her husband, Irv Turetsky.

My folks stayed in touch with them till Abe and Sadie died. To all these Brooklyn cousins, my mother was called Gussie. Oh, how she hated that name.

Years later, when we rented a house for the summer in Long Beach, Long Island, Uncle Izzy came to spend two weeks with us while recuperating from a heart attack. I was thirteen years old and had become very fond of him. Since I didn't have any real uncles or aunts here in the USA, I pretended that he was like a real uncle to me, but he died when I was fourteen, while we were in Israel, and we were unable to go to his funeral. I still think about him now and then.

I remember that he was on the Duke Diet, which consisted of plain, boiled rice and fresh fruit. That was the prescription for heart patients in those days. He was not even sixty when he died. We have come a long way in cardiology since then.

My mother had another cousin on the Lower East Side, another butcher in the family. She did a lot of research looking for him. It took her a long time to finally locate his butcher shop on Delancey Street, and she finally made her way down there to meet him.

By the time my mother found her cousin, he was no longer alive. No sooner had she introduced herself to his widow, she got the boot. Her cousin, the woman's husband, had died shortly before my mother had shown up. My mother just wanted to meet him, but his widow was afraid that all she wanted was a handout. Little did she know that Gisa would rather scrub floors than ask for something for nothing.

Her response to my mother was, "Once the bloodline is broken, there is no longer a relationship." She was mean and nasty.

Unfortunately, my father didn't have family here until a cousin arrived after the war in 1949. My poor father lost most of his family in the Holocaust. He lost his mother, two brothers, and other relatives. Many years later, when we visited Auschwitz, he went around looking for signs of his brothers, but he was not able to find them. Only his sister and a few cousins survived. *How sad to lose almost a whole bloodline.*

His sister, my Aunt Zeisel, was in Belgium during the war, then moved to Israel when it became a state. One of her children–a son named Chanan Ofir–still resides there with his children, but the name Miller in our family has no descendants.

Zeisel, her husband, and children, 1946.

Like my mother, my father soon got restless working for others. He had been accustomed to a middle-class life before the war, and factory work was not what he aspired to. Word got around in their circle of refugees that the diamond industry was the place where he could establish himself and have a good future.

He and my mother saved their money, and my father, whom

everyone now called Avram, learned how to cut diamonds. He paid someone $250 to learn this trade. Once he became proficient, he taught my mother how to do the same thing. My father was a quick learner and a good teacher, too. So then they could open their own business.

Avram never liked to work for other people; he liked being his own boss. Not that he was such a workaholic, but he liked to arrange his life to suit himself. When he worked for himself as a tailor, he and my mother would close the doors and declare a holiday whenever they felt like it. He was also self-motivated.

They rented a shop at 7 West 45th Street near Fifth Avenue and took in contract work to begin with. They rented several diamond wheels and so began their venture; they soon became independent contractors.

Cutting diamonds is a tedious process. It is also very dirty work. You can only cut diamonds with diamond dust. My parents would change into work clothes as soon as they arrived at the factory and change back to go home. You have to be very patient and check your work frequently so as not to cut too much.

Often, the workers would mess things up, and on the weekends, my father had to return to the shop to correct their mistakes. My parents worked long hours and hired many other workers until they had as many as fifteen employees. They earned a lot of money. They were also able to save a lot of money.

The rent for our studio apartment on Manhattan Avenue was $45 a month; we had no cars, just tuition for Yeshiva and summer camp for me; however, during lunchtime, my mother would go to Saks Fifth Avenue to shop. Saks had a fashion salon where my mother and the other shoppers would sit and watch the models come out to display their clothing. A much different experience than we have now. It was there that she bought her fancy dresses and shoes. Always the latest fashion.

She had a pair of platform shoes with rhinestones on the heels that I coveted. *What little girl wouldn't drool over something like that?* She had a turban hat made of multicolored silk that looked like a sheik could wear it.

Women in those days always wore hats and gloves when they went out, or else you were not well dressed. She would come to work all dolled up, change into work clothes, and at lunch time change again to go shopping, then return to the factory and change again. Often, she would take a break and go to Vic Tanny's Gym to exercise. She was, after all, the boss's wife. She was into fitness long before others were.

When she was growing up in Berlin, the government stressed gymnastics for its youth, which continued to play a major role in my mother's life. She worked hard, played hard, and was always well dressed.

When I turned seven, my father decided that I should learn how to play the violin like his brother before me. He found a teacher who lived in a third-floor walkup a few blocks away and arranged for me to take lessons. I'm not sure where the recommendation came from, but nevertheless, I found my way to the building by myself, but I had to walk up dark steps and down a long corridor. I got so frightened going there that it quickly ended my violin concert career before it ever began.

I don't think that either of my parents really put much thought into how I might feel when deciding on my future. They made up their minds without consulting me, and that was that. Perhaps no one during that era behaved differently? Parents just did what they thought was right for their child without any afterthought.

I really wanted to play the piano. My father felt that you could carry a violin around with you to entertain friends and family, but a piano, that was too heavy.

I won. My parents bought me an old upright piano, and so I began my musical career. I loved to play. I didn't love to practice, but practice I did.

My friends Fanny and Rachel Kranz and I shared a piano teacher. I played quite well. I memorized the music easily. I could play by ear. I always had a hard time sight-reading. Till this day, I must pick out the notes carefully, but I can pick out the tune easily.

My first piano teacher was Mrs. Grossman. She was quite a character. She was probably middle-aged aged but to us kids, she looked old; I would have to guess between forty-five and fifty. She was a German woman from the old school, living in Washington Heights, where we gave concerts in her home once a year. We had weekly piano lessons.

Every week, she came to my house first, then asked for a glass of water, complained how bad the water tasted, and then gave me a lesson.

My parents both worked, so I was always home alone. When we finished my lesson, I trailed along with her to Fanny and Rachel Kranz's apartment, one block away on Central Park West. There, she would go through the same routine. She'd ask for a glass of water, complain how bad it tasted, then proceed to give her lessons. Fanny and Rachel were not great musicians, but they tried, nevertheless.

Oh, how I hated to hear her gripe about the water. I thought to myself, *If you don't like the water, why do you always ask to have a glassful to drink?*

Thus, the three of us concocted a scheme in hopes that we could teach her a lesson. I'm sure I was the prominent voice in this mischievous act. We decided that we would prepare a glass of water for her before she even asked for it. We stirred in a teaspoon of salt and then waited. We felt that if she complained, at least she had cause.

She arrived at my home, and then the moment arrived when she asked for water. I gave her my brew, and, boy, did she spit it out.

"Phew!" she yelled.

I did everything to keep from laughing. I just continued with my lesson. Of course, since I was one of her prized students, she didn't yell too much. I was also alone, so she had no one to complain to.

Once again, I trailed along with her to Fanny and Rachel's house. They, too, had prepared their glass of water, and the same routine was repeated. However, their mother was home, so they got a scolding.

Another time, poor Mrs. Grossman was pacing around listening to the sisters playing, and out popped a wad of cotton from between her legs with blood on it. We were too young to know what it was for and teased her incessantly.

At our yearly concert, we invited Nathan Silverman, Fanny and Rachel's cousin, to join us. The four of us headed up to Washington Heights on the subway together and arrived at her house very hungry. We invaded her apartment looking for the kitchen. Instead, we found her husband in a nightshirt with a nightcap on. We were all startled. She finally did feed us bread and butter. I don't think she ever invited us to her house again. That poor woman.

Sometime later, my mother found a different teacher for me; this time it was a Russian lady. I do not remember her name, but I stayed with her for about three years. I soon outgrew her and graduated to a more advanced teacher. He was the best, but we soon moved from Manhattan, and my musical career took a turn for the worse. Had we lived in the city longer, my career might have taken another path, but that is another life.

NINE

Latchkey Kid

I was a latchkey child. I hated coming home to an empty apartment. The apartment was small, but it always felt empty. It faced the back courtyard, so it was often dark, and as soon as I walked in, I had to turn on the lights.

At eight, not only was I left to my own devices in the afternoons, but my parents often went out in the evening, leaving me alone. I had specific instructions never to open the door for anyone.

I still remember the time their best friends Rika and Karl Gittman came to call on them, and I wouldn't open the door. They banged and rang the bell, but I told them that I wasn't allowed to open the door; they understood and left. Lucky for my parents, I was mostly an obedient child. Still, it was both scary and lonely to be on my own.

Looking back, I don't blame my parents. They were immigrants trying to build a life in America. They didn't think about the repercussions. I was in an apartment building with a doorman, so they assumed I was safe.

I liked our doorman. His name was Scotty; he was a big, black man with a warm heart. When I got frightened of being alone, I went down and sat with him in the lobby. I often had belly aches and wondered why. It wasn't until I was an adult and in therapy that I realized why I suffered as a child. Being left alone was enough to make many a child complain of the same symptoms.

I'm sure my parents didn't understand what was going on in my head. They wanted to have a good time and felt that I was safe in our home.

Eventually, they bought me a radio, and that became my babysitter. My parents thought that it would be helpful for me to have a radio to keep me company and help me fall asleep. For the most part, it worked. To this day, I still fall asleep listening to the radio or the voices on TV. It lulls me to sleep.

I had a few friends in the building, Florence Warshawsky, who lived across the hall from us, and Carol Trachtenberg, who lived on the ground floor. Carol's father was our family doctor, and they owned the first television set I ever watched. It was 1943, and no one else that I knew had a TV. Carol was a little younger than I, but I was encouraged to play with her since her father was a doctor. In those days, doctors were very highly revered, as they still are.

On weekends, my father and mother would often have to go to the shop to redo what their workers had messed up during the week. This was wartime; everyone worked quickly; no room or time for errors. People earned their pay by piecework. The more you produced, the more money you earned.

My father had to check the work they finished. He was the quality controller. He generally did that on Saturdays or even on Sundays, depending on how busy they were.

In the winter, when I was alone on weekends, I would read in bed for a while, then close my folding cot, get dressed, take my ice skates, and head for the Rockefeller Center ice skating rink. On the subway, I had specific instructions to sit near the conductor of the train and not to speak to strangers. So much trust, so much responsibility for an eight-year-old. It was overwhelming.

I eagerly looked forward to skating every winter. I longed for figure skating lessons, but my father would say, "First learn how to skate straight, then we'll see."

I admired a little girl whose father was an instructor, who went out into the center and spun around and did all kinds of fancy steps. I would go around the rink for hours while watching her in awe.

My mother did, however, make me beautiful skating skirts. In those skirts, a heavy sweater, a hat, and gloves, I tried to strike a pose as a dancing ice skater. Instead of me getting figure skating lessons, I gave figure skating lessons to my daughter Jill when I could ill afford them. I lived my skating life through her, but as much as I love Jill, she was no Sonja Henie, but we had fun together. After skating all alone, I would return to my father's shop, and then my parents and I would go out to eat dinner.

We dined at several places, among them Gluckstern's, a kosher restaurant, Farm Food, a vegetarian restaurant, and Horn & Hardart, an "automat." I think the most fun for a child was Horn & Hardart. It was a cafeteria-style, self-service restaurant. You found a table for yourself, and there were two different ways to get your meal.

All the hot food was at a counter behind a glass partition, and you pointed to what you wanted, and someone would put it on a plate and hand it to you. If you wanted a sandwich or dessert, they had little glass compartments filled with all kinds of goodies. You had to put money into a slot and turn a knob, and boom–a window popped open, and you could retrieve what you so desired. If you wanted coffee, there was a metal lion with a big mouth that spouted coffee. It was magical for a kid. All you needed were a lot of nickels, and you could have a great time.

I also remember going to another Jewish-style restaurant on West 45th Street named Poliakoff's Strictly Kosher Jewish Restaurant. The reason I recall that place was that I went there once with just my father. My mother had gone to the hairdresser for a permanent, and we were on our own. My father loved calf liver, so we ordered liver steaks. One for each of us, even though the portions were humongous.

My father had a large capacity for food and a fast metabolism. He then placed a bet with me on who could eat more liver and eat the fastest. What I remember is that for many, many years after that, I could never look at a liver steak again. In those years, no one equated eating a lot of food with getting fat. My father would often bet with me as to who could eat more, never realizing the consequences. Later on in life, he chastised himself for this nonsense.

Whenever there was a new show at Radio City Music Hall, we would attend. They always had a stage show and then a movie. If there was an ice-skating extravaganza at the neighboring Roxy Theater, we also went. My father's favorite, however, was to go to the newsreel theater on 50th Street, just down the way from Radio City. We would sit for hours watching the reel over and over. There was no time slot to enter and leave, as there is today. You could sit there for as long as you wished.

We also went to the movies together. I hated the mushy love scenes. I would scrunch down in my seat or cover my face with a hat and ask, "Is it over yet?" There were no movie ratings like there are today. The only rating was whether my mother wanted to see the movie or not.

My mother loved the movies; she even went during our escape in France. Often, she would go by herself, buy chocolates, and spend an afternoon in the darkness of the theater all alone.

By the time third grade came along, my parents moved me to another school once again. I went to another Yeshiva closer to home, the Jewish Community School on 76th Street near Central Park West. No more subway rides for me. I now rode in a limousine every morning and afternoon. I had come up in the world.

Gilda's class at Jewish Community School, 1944.

There were no school buses for the Yeshiva, so the school hired a limo to transport the few children who lived too far away to walk to school. I stayed there for two years.

My mother felt that my English education was lacking at this point, so I transferred to public school; P.S. 93 was the school of choice. I lived out of the district, so we had to use our friends the Gittmans' address. For grades 5 and 6, I now had to walk to Amsterdam Avenue, then take a bus uptown to 93rd Street. It was a long walk; city blocks are very long. Furthermore, I couldn't invite anyone to my house, since we were now living a lie.

I also went to Beth Hillel Hebrew School three afternoons a week; it was close to my school. I finally made a friend there who was also in my class in public school, Ruth Silbiger. We became fast friends. Our fathers were both in the diamond business, so it was more comfortable. I remember we would hold hands as we walked from public school to Hebrew school, skipping along the way. This was something new for me. I imagine that we looked like we had been friends for a long time; we bonded immediately.

Our friendship lasted until 1949, when I turned fourteen and we moved to Kew Gardens Hills in Queens. We then went our separate ways until after getting married. Coincidentally, she also moved to Kew Gardens Hills and bought a house right across the street from my parents.

The war years brought hardships for many. Since we were happy to be here in America, I don't think that there were too many complaints. We had to endure rationing. We used coupons for coffee, sugar, butter, meats, gasoline, and other items I can no longer remember. Since we didn't own a car, gas rationing did not affect us. However, I do remember air raids. They frightened me.

We had to have blackout shades, go through air raid drills; air raid wardens were all over the place. I remember search lights glimmering in the sky. It was kind of scary for me since I had experienced some of the same things while running away from Hitler in France.

In France, I often had to carry a gas mask. That's something a child never forgets. I also remember the numerous drills at P.S. 93 where they took us out into the hallways, sat us on the floor, and made us cover our heads. To this day, I still have nightmares about these air raids.

In the fifth grade, there was a girl whose name was Jill Williams. I always admired her from afar. She had long, blond, wavy hair, blue eyes, and a little button nose. I always said that if I ever had a little girl, I would name her Jill. So now you know the rest of that story.

I passed many a Saturday afternoon listening to WQXR on the radio, hearing the opera broadcast from the Metropolitan Opera House. I loved listening to these operas, even though I had no clue what they were singing about. I guess I just loved the music.

Back in Liege, I'd attended the opera with my mother and her best friend, Sala Rothstein, who was an aficionado and could recite all the libretti. There were no babysitters, so there I was at the young age of three going to the opera.

While listening to an opera broadcast, I would draw. At first, I copied the funnies in the *Daily News*, and soon began drawing girls dressed in different costumes. It seems that my mother took notice, because she went to speak to the principal at my junior high school to ask her if she could recommend an after-school art program. Thus, art became a very important part of my life. It has become an integral part of my psyche, and to this day, it's part of my DNA.

Every Saturday during the school year, I would walk to Broadway, where I would catch the bus and go to my art classes. I had to learn all about buying oil paints, canvases, brushes, etc. Each week, there would be a model that we would have to draw or paint. Right from the start, my instructors threw me into the fray. I hopped on the art train and am still riding it.

When we moved to Queens when I was fourteen, my mother found another art school for me to attend in the evenings. I'd take a bus to Jamaica, where I kept on painting.

I still remember the day I had to draw my first male nude model. I was fifteen and had never seen a naked man. We were very naïve in those days. Here I was, this innocent young girl, and in walks the model wearing only a jock strap. Well, you can well imagine that I didn't know where to look. I had never seen a jock strap and didn't even know what it was. I was mortified and embarrassed by the whole thing. I wouldn't dare say anything, not wanting to look too stupid. I kept on painting and painting.

I finished a whole piece in that one night since I couldn't take my eyes off him.

During the summer of 1945, my parents rented an apartment in Far Rockaway, on the Rockaway Peninsula at the southern edge of Queens. All their friends and their children spent the summer there. It was a happy time for us. We had an apartment on the first floor in a huge frame house with a covered porch. On rainy days, we played there for hours on end. On sunny days, we went to the beach. At ten years old, I had my playmates Fanny, Rachel, and their cousin Nathan. We roamed the streets freely, swam in the ocean, and just had a lot of clean fun.

In the evenings, our folks would get together, go for ice cream sundaes, and just hang around and socialize. For my tenth birthday, I got a bicycle. Since no one manufactured bicycles during the war years, what an event that was. But my father was determined to find one and stood in line for hours. I had learned how to ride at age seven, so I needed a more grown-up bike. How proud I was of this bike. I rode it around wherever I could. My father also got a bike, so we could ride together.

I also got a diamond ring as a birthday gift that year. It was like an engagement ring, just 20 points and two little stones on the side. *How excited can one little girl get?* The sun-soaked days were fun, and the gifts were great, but the most memorable part of that summer was the end of the war.

Gilda, age 10.

It was August of 1945 when the news broke over the radio; I remember going out on the porch, banging pots and pans, and seeing people driving around in the streets honking their horns and whooping and yelling. Maybe there would be peace in the world. A child's wish had come true.

Perhaps now we could live a normal life, whatever that was. No more rationing, no more air raid drills, and no more futile deaths. Finally, the war was over.

But our joy was tempered by devastating news from Poland. We learned that my mother's father, Chaim, her sister, Mitsche, and Mitsche's young child had all been killed by the Nazis.

In the years after my mother's visit to Lancut, Mitsche, who had faithfully assumed her mother's responsibilities after her premature death, married and bore twins, but tragically, one of them died after a year. Not long after the baby's death, Mitsche's husband ran off with her dowry money of 2000 Zloty (about $500), never to be heard from again, leaving her and her young child penniless.

It was 1939, and my grandfather Chaim was in Palestine visiting his sons, Zalmon and Zanvil. When Chaim learned what had happened to Mitsche, he immediately returned to Lancut to help care for his daughter and grandchild.

Chaim Yosef leaving Israel, 1939.

Sadly, not long after, the Nazis invaded Poland. Mitsche and her young child were rounded up and sent to the Auschwitz concentration camp, where they were both killed. My grandfather, Chaim, was shot and killed in the streets of Lancut while rummaging through garbage cans for food.

Fortunately, my mother's sister Chaya had managed to flee Poland. At the start of the war, her husband, Yumen, was sent to a labor camp in Lvov, Russia. Desperate to be with him, Chaya left Lancut on foot with her young son Benny in tow.

Dozens of Jews were attempting to leave Poland. Along the way, she encountered a peasant with a horse and buggy and offered her gold chain as payment to take them across the border. To Chaya's surprise, when she stepped off the buggy at the Czechoslovakian border, the man handed her necklace back to her, telling her she would need it to support herself.

Somehow, she made her way to a train station, where she and her son hid out in an abandoned train car for nearly a month before setting off the rest of the way. Eventually, they came upon a small Russian village, where miraculously they found Yumen, who was working as a cook. Another miracle.

When Yumen was moved to another labor camp in Siberia, Chaya and Benny traveled to Siberia as well. As my cousin Benny tells it, he became the man of the house at age five. In Siberia, he and his mother lived in an attic without any amenities and managed to survive for the duration of the war.

Benny eventually came to America in 1959 to study electrical engineering at New York University. He now lives in Florida with his second wife, Sally. His son Bruce also lives in Florida with his second wife Adina, and his daughter Lisa lives in Colorado, just outside of Boulder, with her husband Jonathen and daughter Ruby.

TEN

Back to Europe

In 1946, during the 6th grade, my parents decided to go back to Belgium to see if they could retrieve any of their belongings and to see what remained of my father's business. With the war over, many people returned to their homelands to see what they could salvage.

My Uncle Hersh and his family had remained in Casablanca during the war years and also wanted to return to Belgium, their home before the war. My cousin Gusta and her fiancé Max were now married and had a five-year-old son, Elias. They, too, had returned to Belgium.

Max's parents had remained in Belgium and were hidden during the war by righteous Gentiles. They had lost everything and were not able to retrieve their leather goods business, so they had to start from the ground up. They soon became very successful once again.

That April, my parents and I traveled aboard a ship called the SS Ernie Pyle, named after a war correspondent. It was a converted troop ship, and we departed New York headed for Belgium. We crossed the Atlantic with my parents' friends, who had two children, so I had company. In the days before Dramamine, I too suffered from seasickness. My mother was even worse. *Remember her crossing to the U.S.?*

Our first stop on this return voyage was Le Havre, France. We stayed in port for one day, and what a fun day it was. There were American soldiers all over the place. Upon sighting "American" children–although I was born in Belgium, I was now an American–they were so thrilled that they couldn't do enough for us. They took us on jeep rides, gave us Coca-Cola, chewing gum, and chocolate. *What fun for a 10-year-old!*

It was April, no school; how happy can you get? My mother had taken me out of school with the principal's permission. He thought that travel was as good an education as being in the classroom, so here I was on an educational vacation.

One of my strongest memories of that trip was an incident that took place when we finally arrived in Antwerp, Belgium. I was carrying a small, white handbag where I kept whatever a little girl keeps. Just before disembarking, my mom grabbed the bag and filled it with something that made it very, very heavy. I complained about the weight, and I wanted to know what was in there.

"Don't ask questions, just give this to your cousin Gusta when you get off the boat," was her reply.

It wouldn't be until many years later that I found out I had been part of a smuggling act. What was so heavy was a solid gold brick. In those years, people tried all kinds of schemes to make a buck. The gold brick was a good way of transporting wealth. Thank God, my smuggling days came and went without incident.

When we arrived in port, Gusta took my white pocketbook and off she went. I'm not sure if there had been any communications beforehand, but that is part of our family history. If they did communicate, they referred to dollars as *"lukshin"* (Yiddish for noodles). It was a good ploy. When they did speak on the telephone, Yiddish words were their secret code. I'm sure there were many others.

Things were chaotic in Europe during those times as people tried to reestablish a "normal" existence.

Uncle Hersh and his family had returned to Brussels from Casablanca shortly before we did. They brought their dog Colonel along with them. I had always wanted a dog, but my father used to say, "When you are older and have your own place, you can get one." He would then relate the story of how he had a dog when he was young.

That dog used to run around freely in his home. One Friday, as my grandmother was preparing for Shabbos, she laid out the meat that she was going to cook for the Sabbath. She salted it on a wooden board to make it "kosher" and then went about her business.

Upon her return, she found an empty salting board but a dog with a full belly. They beat the dog, so I was told, and went on to have a meatless Sabbath. He remembered that story for the rest of his life. So, you can imagine that my wanting a dog didn't bode well. Thus, this dog Colonel became my favorite buddy.

I thought he was so clever and so smart. He understood French and Yiddish. In Casablanca, he was the watchdog at my uncle's fur factory. No one could enter with Colonel on guard. His only master was my uncle, and only he could allow strangers into the workplace.

While in Belgium, my father conducted his diamond business and traveled back and forth between New York and Brussels. My mother and I rented a room in a residential hotel in the heart of town. I felt very grown-up during that time.

Gisa and Gilda in Liege, 1946.

In Europe, there was food rationing after the war. One of the coveted items on the list was chocolate. My mother was a chocoholic until her dying day. Every month, we were given the ration of a kilo of chocolate, my mother's favorite Côte d'Or. My mother promptly ate hers and coveted mine. I would eat a small piece whenever I had the desire for sweets. Remember, I used to bring home my chocolate bars when I attended preschool in Liege. (And my mother thought that she was raising a stupid child!) She suggested that when I get my ration that I should hide it from her.

We were staying in a residential hotel with not too many nooks and crannies. We did have a large armoire in the room since in Europe, they did not have built-in closets. I got my kilo of chocolate and wrapped it up carefully in newspaper, and when my mother was not around, I clambered up onto the armoire and stuck it in the farthest corner, so it would be hard to reach. One day, when I had an urge for some sweets, I got onto a chair and reached up for my hidden treasure to find that it was all gone. Not even a scrap of paper was evident. My mother had gobbled it all up.

She stole candy from her baby!

During our stay in Belgium, we returned to Liege, our home before the war. There, we were reunited with some of our old friends, including Sala and Bernard Rothstein. The Rothsteins had left Belgium together with us, but they had returned to Liege during a quiet time, a "false peace," as did many others.

Sala, Bernard, and Esther Rothstein, Liege, 1947.

Sadly, Sala and her sister were caught in a roundup by the Nazis and spent the rest of the war in Auschwitz, just like my aunt Mitsche and her young son. The sisters were fortunate to survive. Sala's husband and their eleven-year-old daughter managed to escape capture. He was hidden by Righteous Gentiles, and she went to a convent, where she was cared for until the war ended. Now, the family was finally reunited.

Sala suffered a great deal in the concentration camp, but like so many survivors, she was reluctant to share her story with others. Only later, when I returned to Liege with my own family, did I hear of her entire ordeal. Before then, it was too raw and too painful to look back and speak of that time in her life. It took many people many years to be able to deal with the suffering they had endured. Most preferred not to speak of it.

We spent several days in Liege, and my parents found other friends who had also survived the war. We felt like visitors.

Belgium had not been bombed too much; still, there was plenty of rubble left over from the attacks. With people desperately trying to re-establish their lives as they had been before the war, everything was chaotic.

During our visit, we went by our old house, which was behind my father's tailoring shop. The shop was still standing. But we didn't go inside. Five years had passed, but I still looked to see if perhaps my kitten was there. Of course, I didn't see it.

My parents didn't learn until many years later that no sooner had we fled Liege at the beginning of the war than the mayor of the city came to our house and confiscated everything. The one thing my mother lamented was the loss of an oil painting that she had commissioned of me.

We learned that the mayor had met with a deserved fate for his thievery; he was strung up by his feet and killed, like Mussolini.

My father had dreamt of returning to his former life in Belgium, but he had become too Americanized during his five years in the U.S. He now found the pace in Belgium was too slow. In New York, he had changed his profession once again. He decided that he didn't want to deal with the unions, so he sold his shop and learned how to become a diamond dealer. He believed it was a cleaner business and required less physical work. He had his ups and downs while learning and had some losses, but was much happier in this line of work.

My mother no longer went to work in the shop and became a "lady of leisure," at least for the time being.

In addition to his work as a diamond dealer, my father also got involved in the import and export business, traveling back and forth to the U.S. and Belgium. He had a partner in New York, Mr. Littman. (In those days, people never called each other by their first names. It was always formal. Mister this or Misses that. So, I never knew his first name.)

My father was the salesman, and Mr. Littman was the buyer. There were so many fiascos, like the time that Mr. Littman shipped only left shoes and leather bombardier jackets that were missing a sleeve and other such wonders. However, they did manage to make some money.

My father soon tired of the many problems he was encountering with the import/export business and went back to being a diamond dealer full time, as it proved to be the cleanest and easiest trade for him. He could now carry his entire business in a small purse in his pocket.

Greater business opportunities were compelling reasons for our family to remain in the States and not try to reestablish our life in Belgium. But an even more important reason was that I did not want to move back to Belgium. I was now an "American," and I was never going back.

It was still very chaotic in Europe. I didn't have any friends there, and I didn't speak the language that well. Everything was different here in Belgium. I liked my life in New York. I was comfortable, even though we lived in a small studio apartment. My father was doing well in business, and we lived a comfortable life. I didn't want to be displaced again.

While in Liege, I celebrated my eleventh birthday. My parents' old friends from before the war attended the celebration.

Back in Brussels, my mother and I had a daily routine. We left our hotel early and went to spend the day with Aunt Esther and Uncle Hersh, who had returned from Casablanca. They had rented an apartment, and Uncle Hersh reestablished the furrier business he had started in Morocco in the attic of the apartment building where they lived.

I often went shopping with my uncle. He took me to the open-air market to shop for fruits and vegetables. Since they were a large family, he would buy food in bushel lots. There were three sons,

Shlomo, David, and Samuel, and their daughters, Fanny, Dora, and Lola, who was now married and had a daughter, Katia.

Gusta was living with her husband, Max, in a different part of Brussels. Their daughter Frieda, now married to a Moroccan man, had remained in North Africa. Eventually, they would move to Belgium with their five children.

With my mother and me eating all of our meals at their apartment, there were many mouths to feed.

In the evening, we played cards. We sat around a large table playing hearts. The younger children watched. Aunt Esther was known to cheat, and everyone would try to catch her. All in good fun. Those days were memorable.

After a few months, my mother was ready to return to New York. It was time for me to go back to school. We had left the States in April, and September was approaching. There were very few ships traveling back and forth across the Atlantic, so it was close to impossible to find passage on a regular passenger ship.

My father went back and forth several times during our stay, and he traveled to and from Belgium on a cargo ship. There were not many planes flying at that time.

Finally, my mother arranged for us to fly back that September on Sabena Airways. She had to "shmear"–give someone money under the table–to get our seats. I always thought that meant she actually had to slip someone money under a table. *I was a child, what did I know?*

We were excited at the prospect of returning home. And I was excited at the prospect of flying on an airplane for the first time. But it was not to be. My mother went to pick up our tickets at Sabena and found to her consternation that someone else had given a bigger "shmear," and we no longer had seats booked on the flight. We were very upset, but what to do?

A few days later, as was our routine, we left our hotel room and headed for my aunt and uncle's house. No sooner had we walked into their apartment than my aunt grabbed and hugged us. She cried tears of joy, then showed us the morning paper. The plane that we had been scheduled to fly on had crashed in Newfoundland. We learned that the woman who had given a larger bribe and was given our seats was lucky to be alive; she had burns all over her hands. That was a disaster, as she was a pianist. From that day forth, my aunt felt that we were newborn people and were just plain lucky.

Now, how to get back to New York? Once again, my mother had to hunt around for a new means of transport. The only boats leaving Belgium were cargo ships, and they would not take women or children, since there was no doctor on board.

Somehow, my mother managed to book us passage on a ship out of Copenhagen, Denmark, at the beginning of December. We took a train through Europe into Denmark, and we disembarked from there. The journey took about three days and three nights. What an adventure!

In the meantime, the weather was turning cold, and we hadn't packed any winter clothes. No coats, no outerwear, just warm weather clothes. Since readymade garments were not de rigueur, off we went to a tailor. I got a coat with a rabbit fur-lined hood. That was exciting! Actually, I ended up sleeping in that coat most of the train ride to Denmark.

Let me not forget my meeting with my cousin Benny. During those last few weeks of our sojourn, my mother heard that her sister Chaya and her family were now ensconced in a refugee camp in Germany. Smuggling was a way of life for many, and my mother and her brother Hersh gathered as much money as they could, and with great secrecy, they were able to pay a smuggler to get Chaya, her husband Yumen, and their son Benny out of Germany. My uncle Hersh had forged some documents, and one night, they just appeared at my uncle's home.

What joy! Now the three siblings were reunited for the first time in many years. Damn Hitler; we were still a family, if not a whole one. The tears flowed, such hugs and kisses. What excitement! What awkwardness there was between us cousins. The last time I had seen

Benny, I was two years old and he was nine months younger. So here were two strangers meeting after so many years.

My mother and my Aunt Chaya made us exchange personal gifts. I gave Benny a set of eating utensils that I traveled with; he gave me a Russian medallion. So, we sealed our bond, and it still holds today. All this happened just days before we left Belgium for Denmark. It was a sad time, but a happy one as well. More of the family was now in a better place.

Our train journey to Denmark took us through Germany. I was shocked at what I saw as I stared out the window. There were no buildings left standing. Everywhere you looked, there was rubble as far as the eye could see. Occasionally, I saw makeshift stores along the way, and people milling around trying to do business. I remember feeling very uneasy; it was very upsetting, especially for a child to see, the whole country was destroyed, and its people were trying to pick up the pieces. People were selling whatever they could to make some money so they could survive.

We slept on the train, and I kept my eyes glued to the scenery. We crossed over the Baltic Sea and finally arrived in Copenhagen. This again was a new adventure. Everything looked different, the food was different, and the people spoke a language I couldn't comprehend; it was exciting.

We used the train as our hotel until we boarded our ship. I remember going into a restaurant and they served bread that was sweet, and meat served with lemon on the side, and my mother and I laughed at this. Going to the pier and seeing so many kinds of cheese being sold and people dressed differently, it was an adventure.

We finally boarded the SS Gripsholm. This ship had once been a luxury liner, converted into a troop ship, and then reconverted into a passenger ship once more. It was huge. I soon learned the lay of the boat and was helping old people all over the ship. Understanding a few languages, I became a guide at the ripe old age of eleven. I was not shy and found it a lot of fun.

Once we got underway, my mother became a prisoner in her bed. She suffered so from seasickness that she was unable to move around. I had to fend for myself. What a voyage. We traveled in the North Sea in December. This was no picnic. One night, the waters were so rough that all the glasses in the dining room broke, and we had to use cups instead. My mother did, however, manage to go to the beauty parlor on the last day to pretty herself up for my father. There were many war brides on board, and they too wanted to look beautiful for their new husbands.

There was great excitement as we neared the shore. All these women arriving for the first time in a strange land, many not remembering what their husbands were like. I remember seeing my father waiting for us at the pier with a large bouquet of flowers in his hand. He was so excited when he spotted us on the deck. We had been separated for several months, and he welcomed us with open arms and many gifts, one of which was a gold-plated bracelet that I still treasure.

ELEVEN

Back to School

Our trip to Belgium was four months longer than we had expected. That December, I finally went back to school. I was ready. I had vacationed enough and had seen a bit of the world abroad.

To say that things went back to normal would be like saying, "What is normal?"

During the next year or so, my mother and father traveled back and forth to Europe several times. My father, Abraham, had become a diamond dealer exclusively and had given up his business of importing and exporting surplus goods.

My mom wanted to send me to a boarding school in Switzerland so that she could accompany my father on all his trips.

"No way," I said. Once I had returned to the good old USA, I wanted no part of Europe again. I needed some stability.

The alternative for my mother was to get our old neighbors, the Lindenbergs, who lived in our building on the sixth floor, to watch over me. I could attend school, go to Hebrew school, take piano lessons, and practice in our apartment on my own, but I took my meals with the Lindenberg family and slept in their apartment with them. This arrangement lasted just a few days. I hated it. They had their grandmother staying with them, whom they mistreated, and I couldn't stand watching it. I couldn't deal with the situation, and I decided on my own to stay with the Gittman family. They lived on 96th Street between Broadway and Riverside, about ten blocks from us.

One day, I literally ran away from home, knocked on their door, and begged them to rescue me from the "House of Horrors," as I called it. Naturally, they took me in, and I stayed with them until my parents returned. I was there for a whole month. At least I was with my parents' best friends and felt safer and more comfortable. Their daughter Stella and I were good friends, too. Best of all, my trip to school was now much easier, and Hebrew school was closer, too.

The next time my mother decided to join my father on his business trip and leave me, she hired her cousin Genia as my babysitter. Genia was a lovely person, but at that time, she was not what I had in mind.

With Genia, I was in my own home, not displaced, but not too happy either. She tried making some changes at home, none of which I embraced. I remember when she brought in whipped butter for us to use, I put up a big stink, stating that wasn't what my mother used. Poor woman, she was trying her best, and I was being a "stinker." What I really wanted was for my parents to be there rather than her. She was earning a "buck," but I couldn't have cared less. I'm sure there were other such incidents, none of which I remember. Later in life, she forgave me for my rotten behavior.

After my stint with Genia, my mother finally gave up on traveling with my father and stayed put with me in New York.

Gisa and Abe, 1948.

I graduated from sixth grade at P.S. 93 in June of 1946 and went off to sleepaway camp that summer. Camp Dellwood in Honesdale, Pennsylvania, was a *fancy-shmancy* camp. We traveled there by train, and the trip seemed to take forever.

The Gittmans' daughter, Stella, came to camp with me. Since she was younger, she was in a different bunk. We had to wear uniforms, and all our belongings had to be labeled with nametags; it was a totally new experience for me.

I recall going to the camp department at Macy's and ordering the various clothes necessary. This was an *American* experience for me. We had to pack a trunk, buy a tennis racket, and all sorts of other camping items. No refugees in sight. Everyone only spoke English.

My mother had gotten the name of this camp from "The Doctor" downstairs. He apparently had all the answers to her questions about life in America.

The camp was divided into girls' campus and boys' campus, and we met the boys for socials every week. I did have a boyfriend that summer; his name was Barry. I was a head taller than he, but nevertheless, we danced together. I always managed to find a boyfriend even at a young age. Even if I didn't think of myself as a "popular" girl.

I didn't love camp that much; I had a difficult time sharing with others on many levels. I had to sleep with so many other girls, share everything, and make new friends. I did make one friend, another misfit named Janet, and we hung out together. I never felt that I belonged anywhere during my younger years. And camp was no exception.

I was always adjusting to new situations. It might be good training as an adult, but as a child, you yearn to be like everyone else. At home, I didn't have a room of my own, I even shared my closet with my folks; I had no privacy. I changed schools and piano teachers frequently. My friends were those whose parents were friendly with my folks.

The few friends I had outside of their circle didn't always live locally. I had two friends in our apartment building, Carole Trachtenberg, "The Doctor's" daughter, and Florence (Flossie) Warshawsky, who lived across the hall. She and I used to fool around on the piano. We would try to hammer out new tunes. At one point, we had the same teacher, the crazy Russian lady. The problem with Flossie was that my parents didn't approve of her family. They ran a cleaning store, and my parents felt that they were beneath our "station" in life. Whatever that was, who knows?

I did make a good friend in Ruth Silbiger, who attended Hebrew school with me, but even her folks were refugees.

After graduating from the 6th grade, I went on to Joan of Arc Junior High School, the first junior high school in New York City. We were the second graduating class there. It was an experimental school. Before this, kids went through the eighth grade in elementary school and then on to high school.

At Joan of Arc, they tried out all kinds of new programs. Social

Studies was introduced instead of geography. There were many other changes. We had classes by periods, like in high school, and they introduced other social changes to ease us into the next phase of our education. I never finished that school, either.

TWELVE

Our Israeli Adventure

In the spring of 1949, we went off to Israel, one year after the State of Israel was formed. Two of my mother's brothers, Zalmon and Zanvil, were now living in Israel. Before the war, not long after my mother had departed Berlin to live with her brother Hersh in Belgium, Zalmon and his family had come under threat in Berlin and had to flee Germany.

Zalmon's maid, Lisbeth, had gone to the Gestapo after witnessing Zalmon's wife, Gisa, throw a Swastika into the fireplace, putting the family at grave risk. That night, after the family went to bed, there was a knock at the door at four in the morning. Gisa went to open the door, and two men from the Gestapo stood in the doorway and asked where my uncle was. She replied that he wasn't there and that he had risen early, as he did every morning, to buy meat for his butcher shop. It was most fortunate that it was Gisa who had answered the door and not my uncle, who was hiding in the bedroom. The two men left.

Zalmon and Gisa realized quickly that the Gestapo would come back later and that my uncle had to make a fast getaway. Zalmon packed a suitcase and, in great haste, went to a friend's house to figure out what to do next. My aunt knew that she, too, would have to make a quick exit. She packed a suitcase, locked their butcher shop, and, along with her two small children, boarded a train for Poland. She would wait at my grandfather's house in Lancut for a signal or sign as to where her husband had gone. It was not easy to communicate. The only way was by telegram.

Gisa remained in Lancut for six months and then returned to Berlin to hide in a friend's house. She quietly tried to sell their house and its contents. The year was 1934, and still no word from my uncle. She did manage to find out that he had somehow reached Palestine and was working for a butcher in Tel Aviv.

My aunt, Gisa, also managed to escape without help from anyone. I recently found out that she was illiterate. She sent all their possessions and belongings to Palestine on a ship. She then devised a plan to smuggle the money she made by selling the house. She left her children with a friend in Berlin and traveled to Rzeszów, Poland, with her child's stroller. There, a relative of hers, a blacksmith, cut the metal pipes of the stroller and tucked the banknotes into them. Then he welded and polished them, so no one could tell that there was money hidden there.

Gisa then returned to Berlin and was able to get tourist visas to Palestine for herself and her two daughters. They were just going on a vacation if anyone asked them. They soon set sail and left Europe while it was falling apart, never looking back.

When she arrived in Haifa, her worries were not over. She had to bribe people in order to be able to disembark from the ship. She almost forgot to take the stroller with her, but soon realized its absence.

It was not an easy journey, but she managed to get to Tel Aviv to search for her husband. Her only information was that he was a butcher in that city. When she arrived there, she asked where she could find a kosher butcher, thinking that one would know where another one was. She told them her husband's name, and a passerby motioned to her that perhaps the nearby shop could help them. She approached the butcher store in hopes of asking about other butchers, and when she entered, she found none other than my uncle standing behind the counter. Another miracle.

Then it was March 1949. My mother was eager for us to go to the newly formed State of Israel to celebrate Passover with her brothers Zalmon and Zanvil, and her sister, Chaya. Chaya and her family had arrived in Tel Aviv several months before us, so there were four siblings all in the same country to celebrate Passover together.

Passover celebration in Israel.

Before departing for Israel that spring, my mother had gone to the principal of my school in New York City to ask for permission to take me out before the year ended. And once more, this principal agreed that travel was as good an education as attending classes.

We left in March for this new adventure. The journey by ship was unending, but the thought of sailing into our own Jewish state kept everyone in great spirits. My father was not with us on this trip, he joined us later. We were at sea for almost two weeks, but this time, a new medicine called Dramamine made the passage more tolerable. There was great excitement sailing through the Strait of Gibraltar. The ship was greeted by many dolphins that swam alongside us for a great distance. This was truly an exhilarating experience, even for a thirteen-year-old, a sight I have never forgotten.

We arrived in the port of Haifa, where we were greeted by some of our family, none of whom I had ever met. They were all strangers to me; what a large family it was. There were aunts, uncles, cousins, second cousins, and lots more. Back in New York, our family was tiny, but here we numbered many.

We were carrying lots of gifts for the family–items that they had requested from the United States. Goods and foodstuffs were still being rationed, so things like sheets, pillow cases, and instant coffee were coveted.

After going through Customs, we all piled into a truck that Uncle Zanvil had borrowed from the kibbutz where he lived, and we drove to Tel Aviv to Uncle Zalmon's home. My mother had been sent to live with her brother Zalmon and his wife, Gisa, in Germany when she was eight, so she was excited that we would be staying with them and their now-grown daughters, Gerda and Hilla.

Uncle Zalmon had an apartment on George Elliot Street in the center of the city. To accommodate everyone, my cousins and I slept on the floor.

Hilla, who later changed her name to Yael, was then seventeen, and willingly took me along wherever she went. I adoringly followed. Gerda, who was now Zahava, was in the Israeli army and didn't come home to sleep every night. She had a boyfriend, Menachem, whom she later married.

In Berlin, Zalmon was a butcher, the same job he had had since his arrival in Tel Aviv. After many years, he went into the catering business and then invested in real estate. Zalmon had arrived in Palestine (then Israel) in the early 1930s after fleeing the Nazis. By the time we were with them, they were living a comfortable life in Tel Aviv.

My mother's brother Zanvil and his wife Alta Levadi (their Hebrew surname) were kibbutzniks. They were ardent Zionists.

They came to Palestine in 1928 in search of a dream. Zanvil was never comfortable living in Poland.

Zanvil, Alta, Eiten, Dani, and Zohar Levadi.

They lived on kibbutz Gevat Hashalosha in Petach Tikvah, outside of Tel Aviv. They had three children: Eitan, about a year younger than me, and identical twins, Zohar and Dani, who were five years old and really cute. I spent quite a bit of time on the kibbutz learning about life through their eyes.

I really loved Uncle Zanvil. It is my belief that had he been born later on in the century, he would have been a hippy. He was my "granola uncle." He was self-taught. He read many books by famous Yiddish writers and philosophers. He did not believe in religion.

In the kibbutz, which operated like a cooperative farm, Zanvil was the peanut farmer. Everyone had a specific job to perform. His job was to plant and harvest peanuts for the kibbutz. My aunt Alta worked in the kitchen and laundry. Her job changed every six months, as did the jobs of others. They had a small bungalow with one bedroom, a living room, a small kitchen, and a porch. Their children lived in the children's quarters and came to visit each evening.

Zanvil (on right) as peanut farmer.

My aunt supervised all her children's meals, especially those eaten by her twin boys, Dani and Zohar. She always thought the twins were not eating enough, just like any Jewish mother.

In the children's house, the twins slept with other children and one adult who supervised them during the night. The twins often switched beds to fool the "house" mother. They were identical, so it was easy to switch beds. Their older brother Eitan slept with his peers in a different house.

The adults ate in a communal kitchen where the food was served buffet style, and you were expected to clean up after yourself. There were no screens in the dining room, just fly paper filled with flies and mosquitoes hanging over each table. My mother refused to eat there, stating that it was not clean, so her brother had to bring her meals back to his own small kitchen.

He gladly obliged her. He was delighted to have his baby sister staying with him. Of all the siblings, they were the closest in age.

At the kibbutz, they had a central meeting hall where they showed movies and held meetings. For me, it felt like camp. My mother was not a fan of this lifestyle. But it was exciting, it was a different way of living, and I enjoyed experiencing something new.

At the kibbutz, you lived a simple life. No fancy clothing, nor any fancy furnishings, just a small stipend each month for small luxuries such as soap, underwear, etc. This was not for my mom. No Saks, no Bloomies, no Macy's, and no cleaning ladies to take care of your apartment.

I forgot to mention there was a communal showerhouse. I remember running out of the shower with just a towel wrapped around me and being embarrassed. I told you that it reminded me of sleepaway camp.

My Aunt Chaya and Uncle Yumen, and their son, Benny, who changed his name to Dov, lived in an apartment in Tel Aviv that had been bombed out during the Egypt/Israel War. The apartment belonged to my mother's brother, Zalmon.

Chaya, Yumen, and Dov had been smuggled out of Siberia into Belgium after WWII and lived in Belgium for three years before moving to Tel Aviv.

To her surprise, Aunt Chaya had found herself pregnant at the age of 42 and wanted to have that child born in the Jewish State of Israel.

Uncle Yumen and his parents had been "green grocers" before the war, so he was trying to establish a similar business in Israel. There were no supermarkets back then; meat was sold at a butcher shop, and fruits and vegetables were sold at "green grocers," like Uncle Yumen's shop.

To help him with his new venture, my parents sent him a very large refrigerator. Uncle Yumen and his family lived in a small apartment in the back of the store; it was not very comfortable or luxurious.

While we were in Tel Aviv, my Aunt Chaya gave birth. The hospital was very crude, to say the least. It was the Magen David Adom, "the Red Cross" of Israel. They were short on help, so my mother became the midwife and helped her sister during this momentous occasion.

My cousin Dov and I were seated in the waiting room, and we could hear all the screams that my aunt was belting out. We looked at each other with horror. We were two kids without a clue as to what was happening. It was very scary.

I recall going to visit Aunt Chaya right after the delivery and found her on bloody sheets. Dov and I were quite startled at the sight. We were both still at the impressionable age of thirteen.

I now had a new cousin, Amalia, born in May of 1949, the first year of the State of Israel. What a beautiful baby she was! I went to see her often and enjoyed watching her grow each day.

March is the rainy season in Israel, and it rained and rained until everything I wore got soaked. However, once the rain stopped, that was it. You never had to worry again about getting wet until the next year's rainy season. That was great!

Passover that year was a wonderful treat. A photographer was hired to mark this special occasion, so we would have a record of the moment. It was a momentous time for the Jassem family. For the first time in many, many years, two brothers and two sisters were all together with their families. Everyone was so joyous; it was truly a family reunion. We couldn't stop hugging and kissing one another.

I'm sure everyone was thinking about the loved ones they had lost during the war. The horror of losing so many family members was too painful for us to speak about. My grandfather Chaim, who had been shot in the streets of Poland while looking for food in garbage cans, my Aunt Mitsche and her child, who had been thrown into a concentration camp where they died. So many cousins and other close family members. It was a bittersweet time for us. We were both happy and sad at the same time. At least we had each other. The only sibling missing was Uncle Hersh, who was safely living in Belgium.

But he was represented at the Passover meal by his son, my cousin, Shlomo.

Shlomo was in Israel because he had volunteered to fight for the Israeli underground army. He had arrived in Israel on a ship called the "Alta Lena" that had been grounded not too far from shore. He and the other volunteers had to jump overboard and swim to safety. He fought during the entire war against Egypt and fortunately was not killed or wounded. Eventually, he returned to Belgium. But later in life, after getting married and having two children, he and his family made Aliya, and they lived the rest of their lives in Israel.

My mother, along with my three aunts, Chaya, Gisa, and Alta, all cooked, baked, and prepared food for our seder and our days-long celebration. There was food rationing in those days, so it was not always easy to find what you needed for such a feast.

My cousins and I had a great time; we were still young and getting to know one another better. I cannot remember how we communicated, but I had learned Hebrew in school in New York, and having a good ear for languages, I must have picked up the lingo quickly. After all, Dov, who had come from Belgium, did not speak the language, but somehow, children, when left alone, managed well. I think that I must have spoken French to him; I still remember some French from my stay there in 1946. Everyone got along, and we had a great time.

My father, whom we left in New York, followed us by plane, arriving in time for the Passover celebration. Air travel was an adventure in those days. It took him several days to arrive in Israel. If I remember correctly, he flew to Bermuda, with a layover in Shannon, Ireland, and then on to Israel. I think it took him about four days to arrive in Tel Aviv. I could be wrong, but it was a far cry from today's travel. However, he did make it to the Seder, and we were very thrilled.

My father now had to become reacquainted with many of the family. It was a real family reunion, and everyone was so happy to be there and together.

Sadly, my days of leisure came to a sudden end. I had missed almost two months of school since arriving in Israel. My mother thought that I'd had enough vacation and that it was time to return to classes. So, she attempted to enroll me in a public school in Tel Aviv. But the principal told her that I would not fit in with the children there. I was too "worldly," as she put it. She suggested that I enroll in private school, believing I would be happier there.

I enrolled in eighth grade at Gymnasium Herzliya, a fancy private school that is still in existence today. It was not easy for me to fit in there either. The English classes were taught in British English. They spoke of the *hearth* and other such British subjects. I snickered at those words. I played the smart aleck American girl. They called me "Chutzpah Americhaiete," and I reveled in my contrariness.

I had a new boyfriend while in Tel Aviv. His parents owned the building that my aunt and uncle lived in. His name was Maier Rinsky. He was about two years older than I. He taught me how to play chess. I taught him some English. We went to the movies and just hung around together.

At the end of the film, when the lights went on, I couldn't believe my eyes. All around us were empty shells from sunflower seeds. Mounds and mounds of these shells covered the floor, and we had a hard time clambering through the aisles. This was their "popcorn" snack at the movies, and theatergoers had left their shells to be cleaned up by the maintenance staff. It made quite an impression on me as I still can visualize that scene so many years later.

While we were in Israel, my father tried to set up a linen business. He had bought this business with a partner in New York, and they had trouble with the union, so he decided to ship all the machinery necessary to make the duvet covers and underwear to Israel and set up the business in Tel Aviv. At that time, there was great turmoil in the Israeli government. Ben Gurion, the prime minister, said, 50% for you and 50% for me in business. The taxes were enormous.

My father said, "No way," and just decided to sell all the

equipment that he had shipped from New York. That job became the responsibility of Uncle Yumen, who was charged with selling off whatever he could.

For a time, my parents thought we might resettle in Israel to be with the rest of the family. Things just didn't work out that way. While they would have been happy to stay in Tel Aviv, I was anxious to get back to America and the "American" way of life, to go to American schools, and to become part of the establishment. I needed to feel like I belonged. Having lived so long without close family, it didn't matter to me as much, nor did it play a strong role in my life. I had learned to be independent. Good or bad, that was how it was for me as a teenager.

Once in Tel Aviv, my father was eager to visit his sister Zeisel, the one who stole my mother's stone marten wrap when my parents went to Poland to visit my grandmother before the war. She, too, had emigrated from Belgium to Israel. She and her family wanted to make a fresh start in the new Israeli state.

During World War II, they had been able to avoid being deported and made a semblance of a life in Brussels. Her husband, part of an affluent Tunisian family, was a slow-witted but good-hearted man. I assumed that his wealthy family somehow had connections and were thankfully spared from being sent to the concentration camps.

Aunt Zeisel had worked for his family as a maid, and that is how the two met. I guess she decided to get married before she became an old maid herself. Her husband's family was kind to her and appreciative that they now had someone to care for their slow-witted brother. The couple had three children: two girls and a son, whom they named Jean Paul. I'm not sure how or why, but they emigrated to Israel when it became a state.

They were living in a refugee camp, and my father went for a visit. During the war, my father was forever sending food, clothes, and money to his sister. I remember going to the post office in New

York with him to send those packages. He didn't have warm feelings for her, but felt a brotherly obligation to help.

We traveled around quite a bit while we were in Israel, spending time visiting all our relatives. My mother had cousins in Haifa. We spent several days there and had some funny experiences.

One that sticks in my mind was a visit to my father's cousins, the Alexandrovich family. They had two children: a daughter, Bella, who was around 18 or 19, and a son, 21-year-old Elli. He was tall, dark, and handsome, and I had a big crush on him. They took us to visit the Baha'i Temple, the gardens, and the environs.

The Baha'i faith is a relatively new religion teaching the essential worth of all religions and the unity of all people. It was established in the 19th Century and is estimated to have about five million followers. They believe in nature and surround themselves with beautiful gardens.

As an adult, I visited three of their temples. One in Haifa, one in India near New Delhi, and one near Evanston, Illinois. They all have magnificent gardens.

In Israel, my cousins wanted to impress me with something different, which is why they chose the Baha'i Temple for our outing.

My mother and I had dinner with the Alexandrovich family. The first course served was hot soup. My mother and I were across from each other at the table when suddenly we heard their whole family slurping the soup. When I say slurping, you have no idea how loud they were. My mother and I did everything to stop ourselves from laughing. I had to leave the room before I burst into open laughter.

My mother also had a cousin in Haifa, Shlomo Levadi, who had fared well financially. He lived with his family atop Haifa in a chi-chi neighborhood. He and his wife had two children, a son, Ron, and a daughter, Ilana, whom I befriended.

Their apartment had a wraparound balcony overlooking the Mediterranean Sea. When you looked out, you could see all of Haifa, which was a modern city for the times.

We also visited cousins living in other kibbutzim and saw how different each one was. But we spent most time at the kibbutz where Uncle Zanvil lived with his family. While there, I had the opportunity to accompany a group of kids on a day trip to the Jordan border, where there was a cable car from the top of the mountain to the seashore. We were a bunch of kids in the back of a truck, no seat belts, no seats, just some straw on the bottom of the truck's cargo bed, riding through the fields with no restraints. We sang all the way. They would have arrested the grown-ups today for transporting kids like that. We had a great time, and I have great memories.

Our stay in Israel was truly a memorable one. We were there to celebrate the first *Yom Ha'atzmaut* (literally *Independence Day* in Hebrew), the first such celebration for the new State of Israel. People lined up in the streets waiting for the parade to begin.

Just as one would suspect, organizing and getting so many Jews together was not an easy feat. We had procured a great vantage point from which to watch the parade, but we had to wait, and wait, and wait; there was a three or four-hour delay. It was bedlam, pushing and shoving; everyone wanted to be in the front. Finally, the procession began, and a certain quiet came upon the crowd.

We were there to celebrate all the war heroes who helped establish the State of Israel. It was an emotional time, and the crowd waited in great anticipation. Everyone was nervous.

Uncle Zalmon got us a good vantage point on the balcony of his friend's apartment, which overlooked the parade route. I wanted to film this great happening, and so did my mother. She grabbed the movie camera from me, but she did a lousy job. She had no clue.

During that same trip, Theodore Herzl's body was brought to Israel, and everyone piled out into the streets to watch the procession. Herzl was a founding father of the modern political Zionist movement. He was an Austro-Hungarian Jewish journalist, playwright, and writer. He formed the Zionist organization and promoted immigration to Palestine in an effort to form a Jewish state. He was born in 1860 and died at the young age of 44 in 1904. There was a great need for the Jewish people to have his remains brought from Europe to Israel, where he is honored with a monument on Mount Herzl in Jerusalem.

Once more, bedlam coursed through the streets of Tel Aviv during the procession. Everything that was happening at that time was momentous; I was part of history in the making. I was just a teenager, but I recognized the importance of this moment.

Life in Israel was so much simpler in those days. Very few people had telephones. If you wanted to get in touch with someone, you walked to their apartment building, stood beneath their window, and whistled. Each person had their own tune, so that you could identify who was calling on you. I was most impressed. (Today, we use cell phones with personalized ringtones.)

Back then, I went around with my cousin Yael. She would whistle her little ditty, and a friend would come out to the balcony and respond, and then let us in by dropping down a front door key, and up we went, mostly by stairs, as not too many elevators existed.

Many nights, there was dancing in the street. People rejoiced in their freedom and the formation of a Jewish State. People dressed simply. Men never wore ties, and their shirts were untucked. Women wore embroidered blouses, peasant skirts, and sandals. Things were informal. We spent a lot of time outdoors, as the weather was always hot, no rain until winter.

They did have rationing for food and gasoline. Every family got allotments for certain things each month. I was a smart aleck. One day, my Aunt Gisa sent me to the store to buy food. She gave me a list and her rationing card to use. When I got to the store, many of the items were not available, so I picked up rocks along the way and filled up my bag.

When I returned home and gave Gisa the bag, she lifted it, and it was full. She was happy, that is, until she opened it up and found it filled with rocks. She got angry but soon began to laugh. I loved Aunt Gisa, but she was very old-fashioned.

Just before my fourteenth birthday, I went to the bathroom and found that I had finally gotten my period. When I left the bathroom and told my mother, Aunt Gisa came over and gave me the biggest slap on my face that I ever had. "That's for good luck," she cried. It was a custom from ancient times, showing that girls were now "young ladies." Boy, was I shocked!

Life in Israel was at a different pace. You ate your big meal during the day and then took a siesta. You laid down on the terrazzo floor to keep cool while snoozing. During the warmest part of the day, you just relaxed.

Things are very different nowadays, both here and in the rest of the world. I guess air conditioning brought about a big change for the working people.

Occasionally, there would be a *cham sim*, a hot wind off the desert. During such a time, you would close all the doors and shutters and stay indoors until it passed. I did experience a few during my first visit there. You tried to stay as cool as possible.

After being away for six months, it was time for us to return to New York. My father no longer dreamed of setting up a factory in Tel Aviv. Things just didn't work out as he had hoped, and he resigned himself to going back to the diamond business. Life wasn't always easy for my parents either. Like Jews all over the world, they had to reinvent themselves over and over, and they picked up the pieces, and life went on. They were very resilient, for sure.

Saying goodbye was difficult for the family. Having had many months to bond once more, we then had to leave. Departing was a big party as well. Practically the whole family came to see us off at the pier.

Cousin Alfred took many photos and then sent them to us in New York. Both my parents were sad about leaving their families. I was happy to be returning to New York. I needed to go back to my "stable" environment.

Our ship's name was the Neptune, but our passage took so long that we called it the "Schlepptunia." We had a stopover in Naples, Italy. My folks hired a taxi to take us around Naples and Sorrento. We then went on to visit the ruins of Pompeii.

One of the moments I remember most about that trip happened while we were touring Pompeii. We came to the home of a well-known poet. Minors were not allowed to enter, which surely piqued my curiosity.

When my mother came out, I asked her what she had seen.

"It was nothing with nothing," she said.

I always remembered being denied entry, so I tried to see it on two subsequent visits to Pompeii and finally found out. Actually, the second time I visited, I was with my first husband, Ronnie. And although I was no longer a minor, I was again denied admission to the poet's house because I was a woman. The ruins, however, were truly amazing. It wasn't until my third visit, right before the COVID pandemic shut the world down, that I got to see what I had long been denied. There were pornographic scenes painted on the walls that even today could keep out minors. Still, they weren't a big deal.

As my mother so aptly said, "It was nothing with nothing."

Our journey from Israel to New York took seventeen days at sea. When we finally pulled into port in Manhattan, I got off the ship and kissed the ground.

I was so happy to be home.

THIRTEEN

Moving to Suburbia

No sooner had we gotten back to New York than my parents decided it was time to move into larger quarters. True, we had a studio apartment for the three of us, but things were pretty crowded. Our Upper West Side neighborhood was beginning to change, and my mother felt that some of the streets were no longer safe to walk during evenings.

My parents began their search a bit farther downtown where some of their other friends lived, but to no avail. Inventory was limited, as construction of new buildings was still limited in the city. My parents even tried to bribe building superintendents and real estate agents, but no luck.

They had good friends living in Forest Hills, who were quite contented with their lot in the borough of Queens, so they decided to follow suit. They had also heard that Forest Hills High School was the best co-ed school in the city in those days, which was another attraction.

At first, they looked at apartments in Forest Hills, but their broker suggested that with a few thousand dollars deposit, they could buy a house not too far away. He drove them to a new development in Kew Gardens Hills, just the other side of the Grand Central Parkway.

There, they saw a fully furnished model home, completely equipped with a full eat-in kitchen, a built-in radio in the wall, a bathroom with a stall shower, a built-in hamper and scale, a washing machine in the basement, and a backyard leading out from the dining room. They were impressed, big time!

Having come from a studio apartment, that felt like a mansion. They tried out the public transportation to be sure before committing themselves, using a bus and subway to Midtown Manhattan, where my father did business, and they were hooked.

They took me to see the house before they signed the contract. When we took the F-train to the Kew Gardens/Union Turnpike Station, I felt that I was going to the ends of the earth. Even though I had traveled all over in Europe and Israel, the subway trip followed by a bus ride seemed endless. On Columbus Day of 1949, my parents took title to our new home, and there they lived for the next 50 years.

I hadn't yet started back to my old junior high school, and since we were going to move in on November 1st, my mother kept me home to help her pack. Once again, I didn't have a smooth transition into school. I started my new school in Forest Hills in the middle of the quarter, and it was a difficult change. I had a lousy algebra teacher to boot, so I had a hard time catching up.

Science didn't prove as difficult, nor did the other subjects, but I really had to work hard to reach the level of the other kids.

I realize now that neither of my parents really had a great deal of schooling, and they didn't have a sense of the right thing to do. They thought of school as just a place where you learned and didn't pay attention to the psychological consequences.

Everyone in our new neighborhood was from other New York City boroughs, so it was not so hard to make friends. Most of them came from Brooklyn, a place I didn't really know except for a few visits to our cousins. There were a lot of kids my age on our block, and we all hung out together at the beginning.

To get to school, we had to take a private bus. There were only two buses in the morning, and if you missed them, you were out of luck. Not many of the moms drove, so we were mostly on time to catch the bus. Occasionally, we tried hitching a ride to school, that is, until the principal, Mr. Ryan, picked us up and gave us a lecture.

Forest Hills High School was very large, and it was divided into three sections. The kids in Kew Gardens Hills were in one section, those from Rego Park in another, and those from Forest Hills still another. And each stayed together within their groups. Classes were divided among all the schools, so you had a chance to meet students from all three divisions. There were some extracurricular activities after school, but soon those were discontinued because of budget cuts.

I joined the choir and worked in the program office for three years. The head of the program committee was Mr. Udane, my biology teacher, on whom I had a big crush. He had the biggest blue eyes ever. I happily gave up my lunch hour to work in that office. Since I didn't want to eat lunch anyway, I gladly suffered.

When leaving school in the afternoons to catch the bus, we'd stop at the vendor on the curb who sold the best pretzels ever for just a nickel, which we dipped in mustard. We snacked all the way home on the bus.

As a freshman in study hall, we had to obey the seniors who were the monitors. As it happened, one of the monitors was Roger Tygier, the son of my parents' friends in Forest Hills. He gave me a hard time in study hall. Not very nice. (Who knew that he would play an important part in my life much later!) I was fourteen, and he was seventeen.

When Roger graduated from high school, his parents moved back to Manhattan, and he enrolled at New York University. By then, I was fifteen-and-a-half and, all of a sudden, he became interested in me romantically.

When his parents came out to visit for an afternoon, he would tag along. One day, he asked me for a "date." He drove out to our house to pick me up, and then we drove back into the city and went to Radio City Music Hall, where we saw a show followed by a movie. I can't remember the movie we saw. Sorry.

Suddenly, while watching the movie, he became amorous. *Wow*. I surely didn't expect that from him so early on. We did become an item, nevertheless. I was now dating an "older" man while only a sophomore in high school.

His parents kept their car in a garage on our street in Kew Gardens Hills as it was less expensive than a monthly spot in Manhattan, so they were out frequently. Not everyone owned a car in those days, so people rented out their empty garages for extra income. Roger took the car out for a ride, bringing along friends, and we all had a grand old time. We dated for two and a half years. Finally, we grew apart. He wanted more than I was willing to give, and so we parted. Maybe there were other factors at work, but who can remember them now? We broke up after the summer of 1952. He went his way; I went home licking my wounds.

After breaking up with Roger, I remained secluded at home, recovering from the breakup. I was then seventeen, which, in those days at least, was not so young. The Jewish High Holidays were coming up, and at the end of religious services, it was customary for some Jewish temples to run a dance for young people to mingle. My friends Shirley Krauss and Estelle Kovack asked me to go along with them, but I refused. I was not in the mood.

My mother insisted that I go, rather than "just sit around and do nothing."

Okay, they convinced me, and my folks drove us to Rego Park Jewish Center. Lots of young men and women were in attendance. The music played, and my friends and I stood around waiting for someone to come up and invite us to dance. There were plenty of "jerks" and "nerds" asking. I danced with some and turned others down, but I was also happy to be on the sidelines.

The band played Latin American music, fox trots, and other popular music of the era. I felt very awkward just standing there, not knowing what to do with my hands.

My friend Estelle handed me a cigarette just to hold. Okay, now I must look sophisticated, I thought. What do you know, a handsome young man asked me to dance! I guess the ploy worked. However, I didn't know how to dance some of the fast Latin dances.

The young man, Ronnie Schiff, introduced himself. He was eager to show me and twirled me around the dance floor. We danced a fox trot, we danced a rhumba, even that one I knew, but when he asked to do the mambo, I froze. Never mind, he just led me around, and we danced around the room. I was impressed. Here was a man, not a jerk. Ronnie then asked me to leave with him. I told him that I had come with my friends and that I was going home with them. He asked if we could just go out for a cup of coffee, saying he'd bring me right back to my friends. I agreed. He offered me another cigarette and, being embarrassed to turn it down, I accepted, and that is how I started smoking.

FOURTEEN

My American Idol

Ronnie had a new 1951 shiny black Plymouth, and I was duly impressed. We went to the Howard Johnson's restaurant across Queens Boulevard, and there began our relationship.

He told me that he was twenty-four and had been in the Navy and was now back in school studying to be a pharmacist. He was attending Columbia University, and that blew me away, too. An older man, a college man, a man of the world, and a man with his own car. *What more can you ask for when you are seventeen?* I later found out that he was really twenty-five but was embarrassed to tell me that since I was so much younger than him.

After a quick coffee, we returned to the dance and found my mother waiting there. *Boy, was I embarrassed!* It seems that my parents had forgotten their house keys and were looking for mine. *Who knows if that was true?* Now that I think back after so many years, perhaps they just wanted to find out if I was having a good time.

So, the new man in my life met me and met my mother on the same night. Sometime later, he told me that once he saw my beautiful mother, he thought that I would be just as good-looking as she was as an older woman; apparently, that was a good thing.

Ronnie promised my parents that he would drive me and my two friends home. My mother didn't object.

We danced some more until my feet hurt. When we finally did go home, Ronnie tried to kiss me, but I was shy at this point. Still, he persisted.

He quickly made a date with me for later in the week. He later told me that his mother was still awake when he got home that night, and he said to her, "I met the woman I'm going to marry."

To which she replied, "You're crazy; go to bed."

And so, began our life together.

The difference in our age didn't stop Ronnie from courting me, and court me he did. He knew what he wanted. He was now a man of the world. He had graduated from high school at age fifteen and went to City College in hopes of becoming a history professor. He found himself at odds while in college, feeling out of place, because he was so much younger than the rest of the students.

He chose to enlist in the service; it was the patriotic thing to do. He was only seventeen. He enlisted in the Navy, thinking it was the best and safest of the services, but since he was not of age, he needed his mother's permission. After basic training, he was tested and sent to school to become a pharmacist's mate, basically an assistant to the pharmacist. They immediately realized that he was very bright with an IQ of 160, and even though he was so young, he was promoted and given authority over much older men.

At first, he was stationed in San Diego, then in Virginia. He was attached to the Marines; he was trained as a medic and assisted in the unloading of the wounded soldiers as they came off troop ships. He never left the States and spoke very little about those years in service.

One of the brighter moments in his Naval career was his ping pong prowess. During recreation time, there would be ping pong tournaments. He was a champion. The prize for winning tournaments was a free phone call home. That was a big deal in those days, as long-distance phone calls were very expensive, so it meant a lot to him. He was ever so light on his feet, and with long arms to boot, he was jumping all over the place. I saw him in action many times and remember well how great he was at this sport. He was so competitive when playing ping pong that I often had to leave because of the angst I experienced watching him play.

Our courtship was rather quick. After dating for six weeks, he "pinned" me. He gave me his fraternity pin; that was a big deal in those days. I was pinned to a junior at Columbia University, and I swaggered in the hallways of Forest Hills High School.

Life became a whirlwind of parties and celebrations of all sorts. During the day, Ronnie attended classes; in the evenings, he worked as a "junior" pharmacist until 10:00 p.m., and then he came to our house. All pharmacy students had to acquire working experience before completing their education. The best way was to work as a junior pharmacist in the evenings for a required amount of time.

We spent evenings watching basketball games and just hanging around. That was my introduction to American sports. Until then, the only sport discussed at my home was soccer, a game that my father had played in his youth. Not too popular yet in the States.

On Sundays, we would go out on real dates. Ronnie picked me up early in the day, and we wandered all over the city. He introduced me to Lobster Cantonese and other Chinese delicacies. He was my American idol. We went to school dances and fraternity functions, and I lapped up the whole mix. Just three months into our relationship, he proposed. He got down on one knee and proposed to me. I was truly surprised.

I told him that he would have to ask my parents, since I was not of age.

Ronnie had little money, but he wanted to buy me a gold watch. My father, a diamond dealer, said, "How would it look if the daughter of a diamond dealer didn't sport a diamond engagement ring?"

My father took the money Ronnie offered, $250, and he added

the rest so that I would get a proper engagement ring. And I showed off that one-carat ring wherever I went.

Ronnie and I got married on April 11, 1954, Palm Sunday, one week before Passover. It was a rainy Sunday afternoon, and my parents and I were late in arriving at the wedding hall. Ronnie began getting nervous since he was never late for anything.

Our wedding photo.

The wedding ceremony took place in the historic Ansonia Hotel on Broadway on the Upper West Side of Manhattan. We had over 200 people attending.

Just before the ceremony began, my father whispered into my ear, "You can still change your mind."

I never questioned why he said that to me at that moment. I think that fathers want to protect their little girls forever.

The only real advice my mother gave me was: "Never go to sleep angry. Kiss and make up before going to bed."

It's advice that I pass down to others.

FIFTEEN

Losing Ronnie

Marrying an American boy like Ronnie was my American dream. After the wedding, Ronnie graduated from Columbia University School of Pharmacy and became a pharmacist. We decided to give up our apartment in Bayside and move in with my parents so that we could save enough money to buy a pharmacy. Two and a half years later, in 1956, our first son, Jeffry, was born. Little Kenny came along two and a half years later. By then, we had moved into our own apartment a few blocks from my parents' in Kew Gardens Hills.

In 1957, we bought into a pharmacy on the Upper East Side owned by a pharmacist named Sam Miller who was looking for a partner. It was in a tony area of the city, located at 1140 York Avenue between 61st and 62nd Streets. Talk show host Johnny Carson and performers Steve Lawrence and Eydie Gormé were among our customers.

When our sons were two and five, I returned to Queens College. Education was important to me; I wanted to hang my diploma next to my husband's. I attended classes in the evenings, but I had to hire a babysitter every other week when Ronnie worked the late shift at the pharmacy. There were just two other adult women in the program. It was very unusual to have adults attending college. Most women stayed home to care for their families.

My father and husband didn't understand why I wanted to go to school. "You are smart enough," they'd say, "you need to be home with your children."

Coming from my father, it was a bit paradoxical, as my mother had always worked alongside him. I wanted a college degree like my husband, and I wanted to frame it and hang it on the wall next to his. Although Ronnie did not fully understand my desire to pursue an education, he was supportive.

But our fairy life would be cut short when Ronnie was diagnosed with a life-threatening disease, Lymphoblastoma, also known as lymphocytic lymphoma, a type of cancer that affects the lymph nodes. He was just thirty-three at the time. It was a terrifying diagnosis, as there was no known cure. We were in foreign territory, but we didn't want to let this dictate our lives. Faced with this life-altering news, we were rethinking everything.

To my surprise, Ronnie confided that his dream had always been to become a physician, but, growing up with a single mother, he was not able to afford to attend medical school. His friend Artie Kaufman had just gotten into a medical school in Scotland, which is what rekindled Ronnie's interest in pursuing medicine.

Our two boys were now five and eight; we owned our own house, and we had a thriving business with a steady clientele. I knew that Ronnie was smart enough to attend medical school, and I did not want to stand in his way. I wanted to encourage his dream, no matter the sacrifices. Still, it was a big decision.

Further complicating matters was that Ronnie was too old to get accepted into medical school in the United States, *and* he was Jewish, another potential hurdle, so he would have to apply overseas. That meant we would have to sell the house, our cars, and the business, and we'd have to pull the kids out of school.

He sent out a bunch of applications, and we waited. Soon, the acceptances started rolling in.

Not wanting to decide for both of us, Ronnie left it up to me.

After two weeks of agonizing contemplation, I told Ronnie we should go for it. I had watched my parents push full steam ahead in their quest for a more peaceful and better life. I viewed this as a fulfillment of Ronnie's dreams and partly an adventure.

Ronnie applied to seven medical schools, and he was accepted to five of them, two in Belgium, two in Italy, and one in Switzerland. I suggested he choose the one in Liege, where I was born. I thought it was a good omen. Our two boys would have to go to school abroad and learn a whole new language, much like I had to do when I came to the United States.

Ronnie left New York to attend the Berlitz School in Brussels to learn French. At that time, my Uncle Hersh and his wife Esther were still living in Brussels along with their children. We had cousins in Belgium, so we had family there to assist him.

Meanwhile, I stayed behind with the boys to take care of everything else. I was teaching arts and crafts at a sleep-away camp in Pomona, New York, in exchange for my children attending camp for free. I was sleeping in the nature hut, where some of the children brought up their pets for the summer. One of these pets was a boa constrictor that managed to escape from its cage, and I refused to sleep there until it was caught hiding in the rafters.

On my day off, I traveled back to Queens, where I enlisted a real estate agent to sell our house. With Ronnie overseas, it was up to me to pack and arrange shipping for some of our furniture, kitchenware, and the kids' bicycles. Even though we were making a huge change, I found comfort knowing that I was returning to a place that I once knew and that family and friends were around to assist.

Once I had completely divested us of everything and shipped our belongings overseas, the boys and I boarded the S.S. Rotterdam in New York, landing in Rotterdam, Holland, eight days later.

My parents' friend's son-in-law was a builder who had sold an apartment to a teacher as an investment, so he was able to rent that apartment to us. It was just twenty minutes from the apartment where I was born. I didn't remember much about the city, but, strangely, I felt like I was home.

We were in Liege for one year before Ronnie became too ill to continue his studies. In between semesters, we had traveled throughout a good part of Europe. Moving to Europe had been an adventure. Ronnie only had a certain amount of time left to live, and I wanted him to fulfill his life's dreams before the disease took its toll.

Once back in New York, we tried to resume our lives. We rented an apartment in Kew Gardens Hills, not too far from my parents. Ronnie went back to work as a pharmacist at a pharmacy in Flushing. My boys went back to school, and I returned to Queens College.

To my surprise, I found myself pregnant and gave birth on my last day of class of the fall semester. On January 6, 1967, we welcomed a baby girl, Jill. There was an eight-year difference between Jill and her next brother, and a ten-and-a-half-year difference between her and her elder brother. Lucky for me, the boys were a big help.

Three weeks after I gave birth, I returned to college to complete my undergraduate degree. Our apartment was now too small, so we started looking for a house. We found one in Fresh Meadows, about seven miles from my parents.

Jill was a year-and-a-half old when I graduated from Queens College with a B.A. in Early Childhood Education. To be a teacher in New York at that time, you had to have a master's degree, so I took one semester off, then enrolled in graduate school at Queens College. My undergraduate studies had been free, but graduate school was tuition-based. Still, I was determined to earn a master's. I wanted an education. I also recognized that with the unpredictability of Ronnie's condition, I needed to be sure I could take care of my family.

Graduation day!

I continued to attend classes in the evenings and earn my degree in three years. Three weeks after I graduated with a master's degree in early childhood education, I celebrated my 37th birthday. Four days later, on July 11, 1972, Ronnie died. It was one day after his 45th birthday. I was inconsolable. Even though I knew he had been struggling to stay alive for much of our eighteen years together, his death was devastating.

I was now a widow with two teenage boys, a five-year-old daughter, and a lot of bills. At the time, I was working as a teacher and the director of a small preschool in Jackson Heights, Queens.

With Ronnie's passing, life became full of all kinds of small decisions. *Should I keep Jill in Yeshiva or send her to public school?* Yeshiva was private, which meant I had to pay. But Jill had just lost her father, and she would be safe and supported at the Yeshiva that both of her brothers had attended.

One year after Ronnie's passing, the school where I was employed closed, and I had to find a new job.

Realizing I had an opportunity to reset and recharge, I decided to take my children to Israel for the summer to visit family. Three of my mother's siblings were still in Israel, as was my father's sister and many cousins. It would be an adventure, I reasoned.

I rented an apartment near one of my cousin's just outside of Tel Aviv. I felt so at home in Israel that I contemplated staying for a year, but my son Jeffry did not want to spend his senior year in another school in another country. He wanted to graduate with his friends. I understood how he felt. I had once felt that same way.

We returned to New York at the end of the summer, and I found a job at a preschool in the public school system of Great Neck, a suburb on Long Island's North Shore. It wasn't easy. I was a widow with three children and not a lot of money. I had to do a lot of budgeting. But that was okay, because I was very practical.

Through it all, I continued to express myself through oil painting. I attended art classes at Queens College and other private venues. To my delight, my work was featured in many art shows, including at the prestigious Soho Gallery in New York City.

The Soho Gallery, 1980 Oil painting by the author, Gilda Zirinsky.

At some point, I decided I was ready to get back out there and start dating. I was thirty-nine, still a young woman. My son Kenny's best friend's mother was also single, so we ventured out together. Back then, being a widow had less stigma than being a divorcee. Still, it was a challenge.

Two years after losing Ronnie, I went on my first date. I met a couple of duds before I found Dan Zirinsky, and my life brightened. Dan was a divorced man with three children of his own.

Gilda and Dan's wedding day, 1980.

When we married, we became a blended family of six children, just like the family in the popular TV show, *The Brady Bunch*. There were my three, Jeffry, Kenny, and Jill, and Dan's three, Steven, Mark, and Laura. Our boys all went off to college, leaving just the two girls at home. Remarkably, they quickly became like sisters, and nearly fifty years later, they remain inseparable.

Gilda's bat mitzvah.

I continued teaching at the pre-K. Dan was in real estate, but his real passion was photography. Soon, he became my mentor, and together we traveled extensively, photographing the world. We went to Russia, India, Israel, and China twice (where we biked the country as part of a small photography tour). We even had a dark room in our home. Life was joyous again.

Gilda receives top honors at camera club, 1998.

SIXTEEN

Reparations Trip

In the years after WWII, the German government began inviting all those people who had fled from their homes and suffered atrocities because of the Holocaust to return. They were told they were entitled to reparations. Many people were paid a sum monthly. You had to apply for this compensation and file many papers.

My mother left it to her brother Hersh, with whom we had fled Belgium, to file her claim. However, there was a deadline, and my mother had misgivings about that. She kept saying, "I don't want anything from those bastards."

While she did not accept compensation, she did apply for German Social Security, since she had worked in Berlin as a young woman and was entitled to that compensation.

When my parents and I were fleeing from the Nazis in Liege all those years ago, I had made my mother take along our family photos. In that envelope of pictures was my mother's German identity card. When she worked as a seamstress, she had to have her card stamped every month to show proof of work. With that proof of employment, she was able to establish that she was entitled to collect social security.

She engaged an attorney in New York City who filed the necessary papers, and every month she collected money, which she and my father used to travel. This was not reparation, but something that all residents of Germany were entitled to, regardless of the Holocaust. She felt that this was the least she could ask for.

Over the years, many of the large cities in Germany continued to invite their former residents to come back as part of the reparation program. My mother repeatedly declined. She had fled from Berlin at the beginning of those terrible years and never wanted to return. Each year when she heard from the German government, she would say, "No, I don't want to take anything from them; my family suffered enough." That is, until 1989, when she told my father that they should go and call it a vacation and let the German government pay for them.

She was given a choice of dates, and the German government made the arrangements. The City of Berlin paid for everything. If family members wanted to join, they were welcome, but they had to pay their own way. My husband Dan and I went along and gladly paid.

That April, the four of us boarded a flight for Berlin. Having never been there, I was excited. Exploring new territory is always a thrill for me. We were met at the airport by a representative from the German government, and from that point on, we were part of a large group of refugees, most of whom were from New York.

We were put up at the beautiful Hotel Adlon Kempinski right in the heart of Berlin, facing the Brandenburg Gate. My parents were given a food allowance and spending money, too. Dan and I paid our own way but stayed in the same first-class hotel.

We spent a week in Berlin seeing all the sights, going on boat trips, visiting the Berlin Wall, Brandenburg Gate, and Reichstag. We feasted with various dignitaries of the city and listened to many speeches, mostly in German; so Dan and I just listened. I shot videos. People didn't dwell on the past. The past was too painful for most.

It had been more than fifty years since my mother had left Berlin, and while she could never fully forgive, she was eager to make the most of the situation; let the German government pay for her trip, one that she regarded as a vacation. She didn't say anything about how she felt. I'm certain that the memories from that period in her life were too painful to revisit.

Instead, she remembered the good times and the many places she used to frequent. She'd always talked about and joyously recalled the *Tiergarten*, animal garden or zoo in German. Nothing was in bloom when we visited, but it appeared to be a nice zoo, nothing special, only in my mother's memories. To her, this place had always been a happy memory from her youth, and she seemed to take comfort in being able to relive some happier times from her younger years.

Gisa and Abe at Berlin Zoo, 1989.

One of the big moments of the trip was a visit to the Dachau concentration camp. My father had always imagined that his brothers might have ended up in Dachau; he didn't know for sure, but he suspected as much, so he was quite emotional during the time we were there. My father never revealed any of his inner feelings, but you could sense that this place was important to him. He stopped at the crematorium and examined it very closely. He had never revealed his pain about losing his family, and it was not something I ever felt comfortable asking him about.

I can only imagine what he was thinking and feeling as we walked through Dachau that afternoon. It was bad enough losing his father at such a young age, but then to have the rest of his immediate family destroyed in such an inhumane way surely added to his distress.

As we wandered around the reconstructed buildings, he became even quieter. I asked him what he thought about all of this, and he, like many of us, was at a loss for words. It is so hard to fathom the Holocaust and how many people suffered and died because of it. We pray that it shouldn't happen again.

My mother didn't speak too much either. Perhaps her thoughts were with all the members of her family she had lost–her father, sister, nieces, nephews, aunts, uncles, and more. It is so painful to look back that many choose to forget.

I almost didn't write about this chapter in my life, in fact, because I would rather remember the happiness than the horrors. Still, we cannot afford to forget.

My mother's family was very large, but a good number of them were exterminated, so I never met them. It seems that Jewish people are destined to always suffer at the hands of inhumane forces.

One highlight of the trip was an excursion into East Berlin. We hired a car and driver to take us there. We had to go through Checkpoint Charlie, which, combined with the Berlin Wall, divided the city into two sectors. It was like in the movies. I felt like a spy going into the enemy sector.

First, we had to exchange dollars for East German marks. We could only get $100 worth of bills to spend there. While this whole transaction took place, we sat in the back of the limo, afraid to speak a word, lest someone arrest us. Our tour guide was well-versed in English, so language wasn't an issue.

Our first stop in the Eastern sector was lunch at the Grand Hotel, then the best hotel in town. Nothing to get excited over for sure, and the food was not much better. It took forever to make and even longer to serve. At least we had full bellies and could go on to further and better sights. We drove through the downtown area. All the buildings were crumbling, inside and out. This part of the city had, before the war, been home to the more beautiful buildings, the opera house and the library, where they burned all the books by Jewish writers and poets. We passed other municipal buildings. There were Russian police all over.

We were told not to say anything derogatory about anything. Everyone looked haunted. We ventured into a department store just to see what goods they carried. Well, you know what? Dan spied a Russian-made camera and wanted to buy it as a souvenir. The problem was we were shy a few marks to complete the purchase.

We asked people in the store if we could use dollars, but everyone was afraid of doing anything out of the ordinary. People lived in fear, for sure. We went out in the street to ask strangers, but to no avail. Luckily, our driver came to the rescue and managed to find someone to accommodate us, and Dan got his camera, crummy as it was.

My mother was able to relive part of her youth while we wandered around the streets. She had grown up in the eastern part of Berlin. We tried to visit the house where she, my Uncle Zalmon, and his family had lived, but unfortunately, the wall that the Russians had erected ended just there, and the building was knocked down. When we found out the house no longer existed, memories flooded into my mom's head. I remember seeing her face, trying to recall the good times.

This house was the place from which my uncle had to run away to escape being put into jail by the leaders of the Brown Shirts. Remember, Zalmon had a housekeeper named Lizbeth who snitched on the family, forcing him to make a sudden departure from Berlin and escape to Palestine. My aunt remained and fled with her two daughters with the hopes of finding her husband in Palestine. Communications were not readily available back then. It was like finding a needle in a haystack.

Sadly, the house was gone. It was now part of the Berlin Wall. My mother often told me stories of life there and how lucky she had been to leave Germany when she did. Imagine a young woman of twenty-one having such strong feelings as to run from the only home she really knew and venture to a new country and a new life. I'm sure she never really thought it through, but she always lived on gut instinct. She was such a force and had such insight. She never faltered, simply forged ahead, and gave me courage in my own life. (We have strong women in our family, for sure.)

At the end of the day, we were happy to leave Checkpoint Charlie behind and return to the Western sector of the city, which was filled with hustle and bustle and smiling folks. Our trip to the other side of the wall was scary, and I was relieved to leave it behind.

At the end of the reparation week, we took a side trip to Austria. It was not far to Innsbruck, where I had visited some years ago with Ronnie and our sons and learned how to ski. It's a beautiful city filled with good restaurants and old-fashioned buildings, just as it was portrayed in the *National Geographic* magazines delivered to our home back in the States.

One afternoon, we dined in a fancy restaurant, and I'm sure we were the only Jewish people there. As I looked around the dining room, I wondered where these folks had been during the war. I often thought about this. *What were they doing? Where were they living? Who had they killed?* I'm sure most of these people weren't even alive during that time, but thoughts often came into my mind about those things.

SEVENTEEN

The Joys of Being a Grandmother

In 1986, the year I turned fifty-one, I became a grandmother. I am happy to report that I now have nine wonderful grandchildren: Josh, David, Jackie, Robert, Abby, Harris, Ethan, Madeline, and Avery. There is a twenty-two-year difference between the eldest and the youngest.

Gisa, Gilda, and baby Josh.

Through it all, I never forgot my roots. When my eldest grandson, Josh, turned 21, I asked him if he would be interested in going with me to Poland to investigate our family ancestry.

"Absolutely," was his answer.

Why not? If your grandmother wants to take you somewhere far, you go. I also invited his father, my son Jeffry, along as a belated birthday present.

I hired a genealogist in Kraków. We chose that city as it was a central location to both of my parents' birth cities. I arranged for our genealogist to pick us up at our Airbnb at 8:00 a.m. and, right on the dot, our guide appeared in his fancy car.

Our destination was Lancut, the city where my mother was born. Our first stop was the town seat, where all the records were kept. After a long wait, our Polish-speaking guide was able to retrieve some family information and gave us a copy of the record of my family, Jassem. It showed the births of my mother's siblings, but she was not on the list, and we never found out why. We also had an address where my grandparents had lived.

Before the Holocaust, Lancut had a population of about 8,700 in 1939, of which about 2,800 were Jewish. There, my family thrived until the war. My grandfather was a butcher, as were other members of his family. A few came to the U.S. in the early 1900s and were butchers here. But no family members are living in Lancut now.

Our next stop was the famous Lancut–or, as my parents called it, "Potocki"–Castle, of which I had heard some stories in my childhood. It was in the center of the city with a moat that no longer had water around it; it is a big tourist attraction. My mother's aunt had once delivered meat to the castle, as her husband was their butcher. She was the mother of my Aunt Esther, who had sixteen or seventeen children and was killed in the Holocaust. My mother told me that her aunt always had a baby in her arms and one in her belly.

The castle is beautiful inside, featuring many historical artifacts and a gorgeous parquet floor, which is actively protected by the museum and requires that all visitors wear foot coverings. The floor is so slippery that I managed to fall flat on my derriere even in slippers. Thank goodness, I bounced back and didn't get hurt.

We toured the city and found the house where my mother and her family had lived, but no one was home. It looked okay. It was painted a pale yellow. But this was so many years later. I'm not sure what it was like during my mother's lifetime. She left for Berlin when she was eight. So long before.

Jews settled in this city in the 16th Century. There was a long history in this location, but Hitler didn't care; a Jew was a Jew. Those who lived here were soon routed out by the Nazis and either killed or deported to concentration camps. That was the demise of a large part of our extensive family. I engaged my guide to find out more about my immediate family. He could not verify how many of my kin perished, though.

We next went in search of other Jewish areas, like the town center, where my grandfather, Chaim, likely conducted business. We went in search of the synagogues and other neighborhoods where he may have walked. The synagogues were now museums, art galleries, and such. I don't think that one Jewish person still lives there.

I then had an inkling of where my family came from. No details, but much to ponder. It was frankly a lot to digest. As Jeff, Josh, and I walked the streets, I tried to envision how things had looked during those times. The hustle and bustle of the market square was now a vision I could look back on. My grandfather, with his beard and yarmulka, standing at a butcher counter, suddenly appeared before me.

I asked our guide if we could go to the cemetery in hopes that I might see where my grandmother Golda was buried; she died before WWII at the young age of 41.

I recently found out that she had developed a sore throat and went to the hospital to be treated for an infection. After a few days, they sent her home. However, she took a turn for the worse and died. I am her namesake.

In today's world, with so many antibiotics, she would have been easily cured. Had she survived, my mother's life would have likely taken a totally different path. But it was not to be.

When we arrived at the cemetery, we found no headstones, just empty plots. The Nazis had ripped them out and used them to pave some roads. I had read about this previously, but had never encountered it. It made me truly very sad.

I had been told that my grandfather was shot dead in the street while rummaging for food. My Aunt Mitsche and son were sent to and killed in a concentration camp, so I have nothing concrete of their existence. There is a small stone memorial with a *'Forever Candle'* for all those who have been buried in this cemetery. This moment really touched me.

We drove around the city for a bit and then headed back to Kraków. It was a long drive, about three and a half hours, so we had time to contemplate what we had seen. A momentary peek at our roots.

The city of Kraków is the second largest city in Poland and one of the oldest. It dates back to the 7th Century. As you walk on the cobblestones, you can envision the history of this place. It has a population of about a million people. It played an important part in World War II.

The Nazi ghetto created by the German government was a staging area for separating "the able workers" from those to be deported to extermination camps. It was never bombed; you can see the city as it was. The original cobblestones, the trolley tracks, the churches, etc. It has the largest square in Europe. It's enormous. The old church, old architecture, the history in front of your eyes. It is a vibrant place with visitors from all over the world. It still maintains a small Jewish community.

There is a Jewish quarter where some restaurants exist that serve "Jewish" food. Not too many Jews, but every night we headed there for dinner.

The following day, our guide showed up bright and early for our visit to my father's birthplace, Boleslawiec, a very small town of about

1,000 people, about three and a half hours northwest of Kraków. Unfortunately, when we arrived there, we didn't have access to any records. The government had moved them to the city of Lodz. Perhaps we should have gone to that city because I believe that is where my grandmother eventually moved. But I didn't think of it until after we had returned to the States, when I found an old photo of my grandmother with the name Lodz written on the back of it.

In Boleslawiec, we went to a very small town hall and got some information from the locals. There were still some older folks who had lived through WWII. Too bad, though, one of them was thoroughly plastered and unreliable, but the other, a shoemaker, kind of remembered the Miller family from those prewar times. He sent us to see the Jewish cemetery, and we found it in total disarray. Headstones knocked over and broken; we were unable to read any inscriptions, a very sad sight. Tragically, almost the entire Miller family was wiped out during the Holocaust.

Our next stop was the Auschwitz-Birkenau concentration camp on the outskirts of Kraków. We went on a public tour with a large group of people. The tour actually began on the bus. As we were driving to our destination, we watched a video. It was disturbing, as it should have been. We came off the bus primed for experiencing the horrors that the Jewish people had to go through. Nothing can really prepare you for what they endured, but you get a small sense of the atrocities they experienced. It has all been cleaned up, but the sign "Arbeit Macht Frei"–"Work makes one free"–still hangs on the gates.

We toured the many buildings. No one spoke. What is there to say but that the Nazis were inhumane. We have had many wars, but none like this, where they burned people systematically day in and day out, killing over a million people in this one location alone.

My family, my relatives, people that I could have had a loving relationship with, whom I might have laughed or cried with, were just burned or gassed to death. Innocent souls, good souls, smart and loving souls, just plain people, all perished because one man decided that he hated Jews.

God help us if this ever happens again. *Why?* That's the question that plagues me. *Why, just because I am Jewish? Why can't people learn to tolerate one another?* It's a question I ask myself often. We all come into this world as blank slates; we can learn to love or hate. It's a pipe dream, I'm sure, as history repeats itself.

We spent a week in Kraków roaming the streets; then it was on to Budapest, Hungary.

The city is very grey, and the buildings are clunky for the most part, very European, very little in new construction that I could see. The Great Synagogue, the largest in Europe, is a must-visit, beautiful as it is. It has a seating capacity of 3,000 people. Right behind it is Raoul Wallenberg Park with the Tree of Life memorial commemorating those who risked their lives to help the Jewish people during WWII.

Raoul Wallenberg was a Swedish architect, diplomat, and humanitarian. He saved thousands of Jews in German-occupied Hungary from German Nazis and fascists during the later stages of WWII. The monument in the park is dedicated to him. It is very beautiful and moving.

We visited the Jewish quarter and walked through the cemetery. That, too, is really old, with so many headstones, one leaning against the other. The city is old and was under communist rule for a long time. So many Jewish people were sent to concentration camps and died in Hungary.

Our old neighbors in Kew Gardens Hills, Klara and Denis Winston, were Hungarian and survived the concentration camps, but like many survivors, they never spoke about it.

I was extremely fortunate to share this experience with my family.

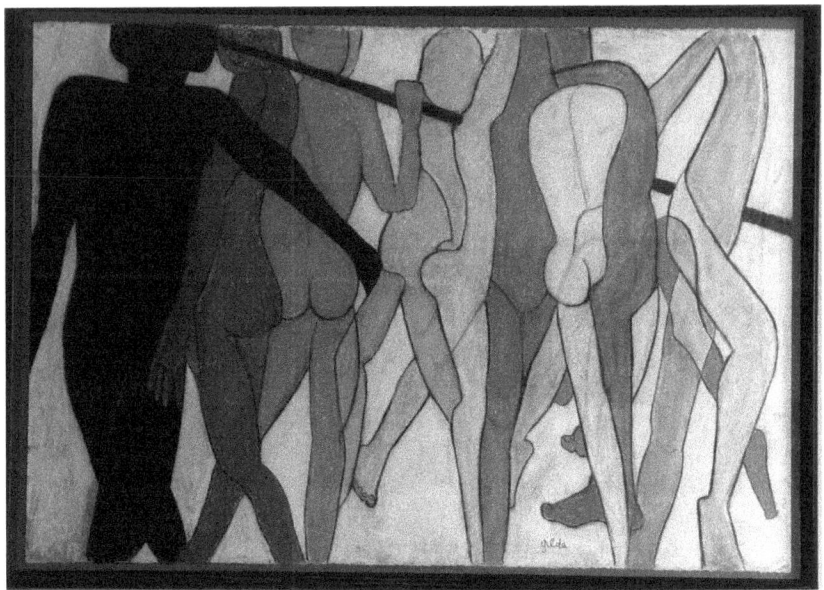

Man in Motion 2010. A man with a cane and top hat came to a studio and danced around. Pastels by the author, Gilda Zirinsky.

EIGHTEEN

The Patriarch and the Matriarch Die

For many years, my parents spent their winters in Florida. They were always renters. They leased different apartments each winter. They moved around a bit, but my father always said he would never move away from his children and grandchildren. Generally, they stayed in North Miami, where many of their refugee friends had apartments. They were snowbirds, wintering in Florida. Back to New York for the rest of the year.

Gisa's 80th birthday.

I visited them in Florida whenever I could. Once I stopped teaching, I could arrange my time so it was easier to see them. Often, my husband Dan would come along. He was always willing to sleep on a pull-out sofa and put up with whatever conditions were on offer. During our visits, we took my parents out for dinners and enjoyed many fun excursions. A good time was had by all. Until....

One year, when we visited, my father wasn't feeling right. He had had quintuple bypass surgery at 80 and was truly ailing by the time he reached 88. My mother and I felt that he had to go to the hospital, where he would get better care than we could give him. We called for an ambulance, and while we were waiting for it to arrive, my father began to cry.

The doctors at the hospital took good care of him, but his heart failed on March 13, 1993. It was the day before Dan's birthday. I remember it well. We were all devastated.

My mother said, "I thought that he would live forever."

He was truly her knight in shining armor. He had come to her rescue in Belgium. They had reunited like a miracle when separated in France during our flight from the Nazis; they had lived through so many of life's good and hard times. He was her best friend, and now he was gone.

They were married for sixty-one years. You become 'One' when you live together for that long. I cannot ever remember hearing them have a harsh argument; they had their disagreements, I'm sure, but they always kissed and made up.

I had a different kind of relationship with my father. He was a man of few words, but I knew he loved me. His death brought back the awful memories of when he had to leave us on the train in France when we were running away from the Nazis and he was forced to join the Polish army. How I had cried.

I remembered how he used to tuck my feet in every night before I went to sleep; how we sat on the floor and played a marble game by cutting little doorways into a shoe box and trying to roll the marbles into the different size "doorways"; when he taught me how to ride a bicycle; the food bets we made on who was going to eat more; when he let me put rollers into his curly hair and we would laugh; and when my mother went to Canada to meet my cousin and she left us alone and made me responsible for dinner. (I tried making potato soup, and it was so thick that the spoon stood up.)

Still, he said, "It's the best soup I ever ate."

Art in pastels of my father, 2025. Portrait by the author, Gilda Zirinsky.

All these small memories and so many more were what I was left with. He always made me feel protected. When I was about ten, I told him that a boy whom I played with in our building had pushed me, and he got enraged. He ran down to the boy's apartment and banged on the door until someone appeared, and he yelled, "Your son pushed my daughter, and I don't ever want to see him near her again!"

Moments like these made me feel loved and wanted. I don't remember having any really difficult times with him. His mantra was, "We have only one child, but a good one."

My mother and I arranged for his funeral while still in Florida. We flew his body home, and the whole family attended. All the grandchildren flew to New York. So many people, friends, and family came to pay their respects. He was one of the last male refugees in my parents' circle.

"Papa Abe," as he was known, deeply loved his family and was well remembered. Sad as it was, he was finally at peace. My mother would have to make a new life for herself, and it was not going to be easy for her.

My mother, the strongest woman I have ever known, had a difficult time maneuvering her new life as a widow. In her early eighties, she still lived in her house in Kew Gardens Hills. I was there frequently, but I could never fill the void my father left. She no longer drove and was fully dependent on others to provide transportation. That can make anyone depressed, especially if you have been independent your whole life.

I would find her looking out the window, blankly wearing a sad expression. There were no Uber or Lyft services back then, so she walked to the market on Main Street as needed.

It was around this time that assisted living facilities were first cropping up, and we found a lovely one not too far from my house. She would spend the next three years there.

On September 4, 2011, my son Jeff's birthday, she died peacefully with her family around her. The strongest lady in the family was now gone. It wasn't until her passing that I realized how much her strength had impacted me and our family. She had always been my role model. She had left home at the age of eight to live with relatives in another country before moving in with her brother and his young wife; she went to school in Berlin, where she had to learn a new language and cope with life without a mother or father to guide her.

I think back, "Where was my grandfather?" He came to visit now and then, but Zalmon, her eldest brother, really took on that chore.

She learned how to become a seamstress and went out to work to help pay her way. She had to become an independent person way before others. Yes, she was fortunate that her sister-in-law was a wonderful person and treated her like her own, but you have to have a big heart to do so. Fortunately, throughout my mother's life, she was treated well by her family. She was the youngest, and I guess everyone had a soft spot for her. She reciprocated in kind. She went out into the world and never let it beat her down.

She was strong and passed that strength on to the rest of the family.

NINETEEN

My Return to Casablanca

In March of 2019, I got a chance to return to Casablanca. My son Jeffry, a college professor, was going to be there for a month, and I invited myself to spend a week there with him. No sooner had I landed did memories flood back. I wanted to search for all the smells that I had stored up since I was a child.

The people, many dressed in hijabs and other garb from the past, excited me. I was going back in time. Even though I had been a young child when I was last there, I didn't feel strange in the country.

I hired a wonderful guide who drove us around the countryside, and it brought back the sounds and smells of my youth. We looked for any signs of the Jewish community that might still be around. There used to be 100,000 Jews in Morocco. King Mohamed V was very kind to us. When the Nazis arrived in Morocco, they went to the king and asked for a list of all the Jewish people.

King Mohamed V promptly told them, "We have no Jewish people here, only Moroccans."

There are not many Jews left there. Many gave up their businesses and went to live in Israel and other countries that were more hospitable to Jews.

We visited a synagogue that is now a museum, the Jewish cemetery, and other touristy places that had been Jewish symbols some time ago. It was fascinating, mostly because of my childhood memories.

Our last stop was Casablanca, where I had a difficult time orienting myself. It's a bustling city, and I couldn't recognize anything. I was just six years old when we left there in 1941, and it was seventy-five years later. We did try to find Rick's Café from the movie *Casablanca*, but unfortunately, it was closed that day.

I thought about all the refugees who were saved in this country. How lucky we and they were. So many people didn't have that good fortune and were so brutally killed. Many of my family members included.

The world is so cruel, much of the time. It never seems to end. *Are we doomed to always kill one another over what seem simple matters?*

I joke often that it's lousy toilet training. It's a pecking order. What evil was done to you, it seems that you need to pass it on to others.

Mannequins 1999. From a photo taken in Egypt. Oil painting by the author Gilda Zirinsky.

Epilogue

On March 27, 2016, my beloved husband Dan died. He was my best friend, and I still miss him every day.

Gilda and Dan at Dan's 80th birthday.

I celebrated my 85th birthday during the Coronavirus pandemic. I am 89 as I write these words, eagerly looking forward to my 90th

birthday celebration. I actually celebrated it one year early in Spain with my three children, and it was great. I am fortunate that I love my children, and they love me.

Celebrating my 90th birthday in Spain with my children.

I hope to live long enough to see how my children, my grandchildren, and, hopefully, my great-grandchildren will fare and someday become who they want to be.

Mine has been a long life filled with so many happenings and adventures. I started boxing when I was in my eighties. I saw somebody else boxing and I liked it; I thought it would be fun, and it is also very good for your body and your brain.

Now, nearing 90, I have embarked on yet another new career. As a Holocaust survivor, I feel it is my duty to speak up and speak out, so that we may never forget.

To date, I have been invited to speak about my experiences at the Holocaust Museum in Glen Cove, New York, and at various schools and synagogues around the metropolitan area. I even did a Zoom presentation to students in Fort Wayne, Indiana and Madison, Idaho, upstate New York, and Boston Massachusetts.

I will continue to share my story in hopes of educating young people on the horrors of the Holocaust while teaching about the importance of love, kindness, and tolerance.

Never again.

Gilda at Iguazu Falls, on the border of Argentina and Brazil.

Me and my three children on my 90th birthday.

Me and my six children on my 90th birthday.

Six of my nine grandchildren on my 90th birthday.

Acknowledgments

First and foremost, I would like to acknowledge and remember all those who perished in the Holocaust; "Never again."

To my wonderful children, Jeffry Schiff, Kenny Schiff and Jill Schiff Monoson, thank you for all your support and encouragement during the writing of this book, and always.

To Laura, Steven and Mark Zirinsky, my stepchildren, I am happy you came into my life.

In remembrance of Ronnie Schiff, my first husband and 100% *American* man, whose gift to me was our three wonderful children.

To my second husband, Daniel Zirinsky, also known as the "very handsome one," who made the second half of my life meaningful, I miss laughing with you every day.

I am forever grateful to the non-profit refugee organization HIAS for welcoming us when we first arrived in the United States and helping us to settle in this wonderful country.

To Captain Snow, who risked his own career to rescue us in Bayonne, France, by dumping his cargo and allowing us to board his ship destined for Portugal. His brave actions enabled us to continue our journey towards safety in Casablanca, Morocco. Captain Snow, there are no words to express my heartfelt gratitude.

And finally, I would like to acknowledge my wonderful parents, Gisa and Abraham, for their strength and fortitude. It was through the writing of this book that I came to understand how strong you both were; it is through your love and example that I am able to enjoy a full and meaningful life.

www.ingramcontent.com/pod-product-compliance
Lightning Source LLC
Chambersburg PA
CBHW061737070526
44585CB00024B/2709